T0001212

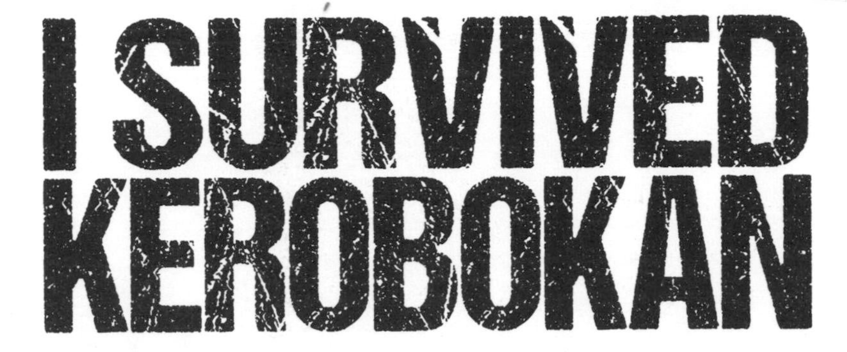
I SURVIVED
KEROBOKAN

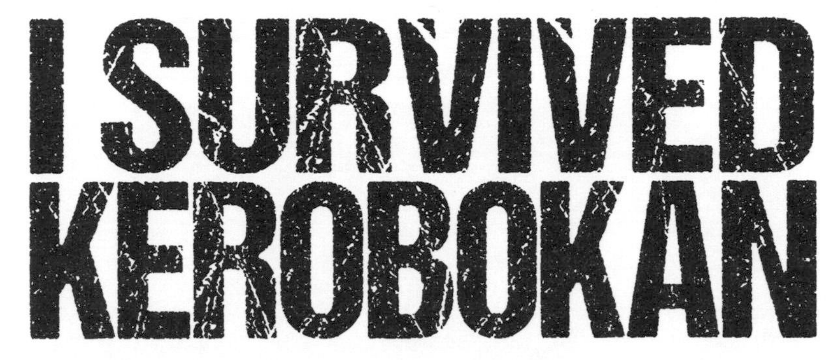

A SHOCKING STORY FROM BEHIND THE BARS OF BALI'S MOST NOTORIOUS PRISON

PAUL CONIBEER

WITH ALAN J. WHITICKER

CONTENTS

INTRODUCTION

I Survived Kerobokan is my true account of a holiday to the island paradise of Bali that went horribly wrong. Although, at times, it seemed like a terrible dream, what happened to me was very real.

Some names have been changed to protect the families of the guilty from further grief and public scrutiny, but all the events in this book were part of my experience of being locked up in Kerobokan Prison.

In October 2012 I was sent to Bali's infamous 'Hotel K'—a home to rapists, murderers and drug traffickers, some of whom remain on death row—for failing to pay a hotel bill after my wallet and phone were stolen by street kids. I spent 58 days in a hellhole of a cell at Kuta Police Station and, when I refused to pay the bribes and 'fines' imposed upon me, I was sentenced to ten months after being found guilty of 'fraud and deception'.

This couldn't happen, I told myself. It couldn't be right, doubting Kerobokan inmates quizzed me while I awaited sentencing. I was innocent! It felt like I was in a twilight zone where civilised behaviour didn't exist and rules of justice were turned on their head.

When I arrived in Kerobokan, no one knew who I was or was aware of my story. Efforts to get help from family and friends had fallen through—a combination of the poor state of my relationships, unresolved passport issues and Indonesian corruption. I received no support for the Australian consulate. I was on my own.

Despite this, I was able to survive in a prison built for 320 people but crammed to breaking point by a thousand inmates. I befriended members of the Bali Nine—the group of young Australians caught smuggling heroin out of the country in 2005—and met the prison's most notable inmate, Schapelle Corby. I watched and learned the prison rules and absorbed the established norms.

And I tried to remain positive.

Kerobokan was actually a minor blessing after the filth of a holding cell at the Kuta Police Station. In almost two short months, my mind and body deteriorated badly after sleeping on a tiled concrete floor with a plastic water bottle as a pillow. The heat, a lack of ventilation and the stench of bodies so close together was almost unbearable; but although the conditions were just as oppressive at Kerobokan I could at least walk around during the day, talk to the other prisoners about their stories and use whatever ingenuity

I could muster to make my time in there as comfortable and productive as possible.

I created my environment and my own reality.

My story takes place in Block B, where 52 men lived in 14 rooms and a common area designed to accommodate 33 people. We were the *bule*s—the Indonesian word for Westerners—and we were crowded into these rooms or we slept, drenched in sweat, on the concrete floor with the rats and the cockroaches and insects. I had no money to begin with and I had to scrape together whatever I needed—water, food and clothing—until my family could send money to me. Later, I gave back to the block and shared whatever I had whenever I could.

The gangs left me alone because I followed the advice given to me by a prisoner I met at Kuta Police Station... don't do drugs and don't borrow money from the gang bosses. I trained hard and tried to keep my mind and body strong, but I avoided confrontation and tried to get along with everyone on the inside. I saw relationships and loyalties tested daily, shifting uneasily as prisoners cracked under the pressure and strain. I also tried not to judge the other prisoners, and in the worst possible circumstances I met people who I will remember for the rest of my life.

Some of the inmates looked like the photos from concentration camps in the Second World War. I could see the outlines of their ribs; they were frail and losing their minds with many years of their sentences still to serve. Many were on drugs or involved in the drug trade inside the prison. Several were beaten to death. One man died in my arms from his illness. I too fell ill and thought I was going to die. I was angry, losing my mind and close to giving up hope.

And yet I survived.

I wanted to write this book to warn people that the real Bali is not the one advertised in the tourist brochures. Behind the obvious attractions—places I took joyful advantage off in my youth—it remains dangerous and corrupt: a trap for the young, the naïve and those, like me, who wanted to have a good time at the expense of common sense. I also wanted to tell the stories of the characters I met inside: the mafia boss, the gang leader, the surfer, the chef, the drug mule, the fisherman and, like me, those who were innocent.

Lastly, the people of Australia, and the rest of the world, need to remember that its citizens are rotting in a far away prison and no matter their crimes, no matter the circumstance in which they found themselves in prison, they are still human beings. The drug trade is a terrible waste of human life and human potential. So is the death penalty.

I was a small fish in an ocean of international drug traffickers; loan sharks who were happy to kill over an unpaid debt or a personal slight and a corrupt prison system where the guards squeezed you of every last rupiah you could muster.

It has changed me, and I think I am a stronger and better person for the experience. I walked out of there with a diploma in human nature, a working knowledge of how the international drug trade operates through Bali and numerous life lessons I will never forget.

This is my story.
Paul Conibeer, February 2014

CHAPTER 1

'WELCOME TO BALI: DEATH TO DRUG SMUGGLERS!'

Looking back at it now, and I would never have admitted it at the time, my life was at a personal low when I arrived in Bali in June 2012. I was 43 years old. Having chucked in my job as a car salesman and ended a long-term relationship with my girlfriend Penny, my life was a mass of loose threads. I hadn't spoken to my mother and brother in the United States for several years and had lost contact with my father in Sydney, despite the fact that I had lived there, on and off, since I decided to return home from the States, where I had worked for almost a decade, in 1998. I was lost, restless and keen to disappear into the alcohol-fuelled haze of the Bali bar scene for a couple of months. So I followed the long trail of Australian tourists to Indonesia's island paradise for some much- needed time out to think about how I had got to this point in my life, and to find out where I was going.

It had been more than a decade since I had last been to Bali.

During my wilder years, before I had gone to the United States to live in 1988, it had almost been a second home to me. The Bali bombings in 2002 and 2005 destroyed Bali's tourist industry and sent many local businesses to the wall, but by the end of the decade tourists were once again flocking to the party island.

When I walked through Denpasar International (Ngurah Rai) Airport all these years later, I noticed that little had changed since I was last here on holiday, chasing the sun, the girls and a good time. The huge sign still greeted visitors: 'Welcome to Bali. Death to Drug Smugglers!'

The ominous warning seemed to do little to deter would-be drug smugglers. And Western newspapers delighted in stories of those who had tried and failed: the Bali Nine—nine young Australians caught in 2005 as they prepared to board a plane home with 8.3 kilograms of cocaine strapped to their bodies, resulting in death sentences for two of them; and Lindsay Sandiford—the 57-year- old British grandmother sentenced to death in January 2013 for attempting to smuggle 4.8 kilograms of cocaine into the country from Thailand. Both of these cases followed in the wake of the international coverage that occurred when Schapelle Corby, a 27-year-old Australian woman, was caught in 2004 and sentenced to 20 years for trying to smuggle 4.2 kilograms of cannabis inside a vacuum-sealed bag secreted inside a bodyboard case. These highly publicised cases of long jail sentences and the death penalty meted out to Westerners did not stop those who continued to go there to party, and, for some, to take part in dangerous and illegal behaviour.

Leaving the airport, I caught a taxi to the four-star hotel the 101 Legian, right in the heart of Kuta. The Legian had a swimming pool, a bar on the roof and a great view, and cost about 100 dollars a night. The problem soon became that I spent almost no time there because I was out partying all night and I decided I didn't want to spend 100 dollars a night just so I could have a swim and get a drink on the roof. After a couple of weeks I found a brochure for a smaller, cheaper place; it was a converted brothel with upstairs rooms around a nice pool area and had been completely renovated. The best part was that it was only 35 dollars a night. There was also almost no one there when I booked in, just a big guy with his *benchong* (Indonesian transvestite) boyfriend, and an Aussie guy and his girlfriend.

I wanted to stay in Bali for eight to ten weeks and put the past far behind me. I was in my early forties, fit and healthy, with no real attachment to anything or anyone. Marriages and relationships had come and gone; money had been earned and spent without any thought to the future and I needed to make a fresh start—again— when I returned to Australia.

But first, there was a good time to be had in Bali.

I had the money and the time, so every night I was out on the town meeting people in bars and having a great holiday. My hotel bill, which was about 250 dollars a week, grew to about 1,200dollars in the last month. I was ready to fly back to Australia, but I met an Indonesian girl and decided to stay on in Bali for a couple more weeks. There was no reason for me to go home—nothing to return to—so the decision was easy. Her name was Icha, and she worked next door to the hotel at a 'charcoal chicken' café. When I first met her she was with a guy from Western Australia. I met them in a bar one night and we all got on well, and when I walked past her workplace a couple of days later, she called out to me. I saw them together later that night—he was drunk and told me he was heading home—and I thought, 'great', Icha and I could get to know each other a little better.

The next day, Icha called out to me again as I walked past and we agreed to meet up at a local nightclub. It was all very friendly and I thought she was interested in me, but as soon as we got there she started chatting up another Australian guy. They hit if off pretty well so I left them to it and didn't see her again for a couple of days. We caught up later in the week and she said the other Australian was texting her and asking her out. I shrugged and told her I didn't mind at all. I barely knew her and I decided just to leave it. She probably was expecting more of a reaction from me than the shrug I gave her, but in Kuta girls come and go. It was then that she turned nasty on me. Walking to a bar early the next evening I saw Icha in the street and she swore at me as I walked past. 'What was that about?' I thought to myself. 'Women!'

It wasn't long before I started getting threatening text messages from her Australian guy, warning me to stay away from her.

I told him I didn't want anything to do with Icha and that he was welcome to her. I was drunk at a local haunt later that week and when he texted me again, warning me to stay away from her, *or else.* I abused the pair of them on the phone, which wasn't a smart move. The next time I saw her in the street she threatened to kill me and spat at me.

The situation with Icha and the overly aggressive Australian was putting a serious dampener on my Bali mindset. Who needed the aggravation? So that night, I decided to head off to a popular bar called the Engine

Room at Kuta Beach, which is a favourite hangout for internationals. I had met another Indonesian girl there the previous night and I knew it was always good fun there. On the road to the Engine Room was the ever-present group of Indonesian teenagers who hung around in the street all night. When I was out in Bali, I usually kept my wallet down the front of my board shorts for safekeeping, but not this night. I was wearing a large pair of cargo pants with pockets on my thighs and I had put my phone and wallet in one of them. This small decision changed my life forever. I remember one of the kids came up to me and grabbed my hand and brushed up against me, asking me for money and trying to sell me something. I took no notice of him but when the group persisted I told them to piss off.

This is when I believe my phone and wallet were stolen.

I got to the bar to order a drink and realised that my wallet was gone. I started searching for it in my other pockets and soon noticed that my phone was gone too. Shit. I started frantically searching the floor of the bar but found nothing; there was no way I'd left it back in my hotel room but after scouring the bar and starting to panic I went back to check anyway. I went through all my belongings but it wasn't there. Fuck! I had about 500 dollars in cash in that wallet, as well as my credit cards and all my personal contacts in my phone. I was absolutely lost without them.

I must have walked up and down that road half a dozen times that night, retracing my steps and hopelessly searching for my wallet and phone. I went back to the bar a second time and asked staff there if they had been handed in. As if! I was desperate to get my cards back because I still had my hotel bill to pay and I needed to access money. I asked an

Indonesian man sitting at the bar if he had seen a wallet on the floor. 'Me no see', he said, and then asked me to buy him a beer. The locals I asked only cared about someone buying them a drink. Even the girl I was with earlier that night, who was all over me, moved on to another guy when she realised I had no money.

I had a sinking feeling in my stomach. I had to get out of there straight away. The only positive news was that my passport was in the office security safe back at the hotel, so at least I still had that.

I went back to my room and slept fitfully for a couple of hours, but when I woke the following morning I knew I was in deep trouble. There was only one phone at the hotel. Guests weren't able to make international calls and there was no computer.

There was an Internet café at the bottom of the street but it cost 8,000 rupiah a minute to use the phone, which was only about 90 cents. I turned out my pockets to see if I could muster the change. No luck. I went down to the café and I told the owner I needed to make an international phone call to Australia. 'Someone has stolen my phone and wallet', I told him. 'I just need to ring someone in Australia to transfer some money to me'.

'No', the Indonesian owner said, 'you pay now!' He wouldn't even let me use the computer to send an email, although it cost just 1000 rupiah, about 15 cents. I decided to go back to the hotel and talk to the management about what had happened to me. In hindsight, this was the worst decision I could have made. I went into the small office on the ground floor of the hotel and told the manager that my phone and wallet had been stolen. Could I please make a phone call home to Australia? He told me to go down to the Internet café to do that. I had already tried, I said, but I had no money. Please could I use the phone?

He said no.

To this day, I don't know why I just didn't go into the street and ask a stranger if I could use their phone, but I think I had too much pride to throw myself at the mercy of strangers. I had been able to talk my way out of trouble all my life and I was sure I could do it again. How wrong I was.

The scene inside the hotel office soon descended into a slanging match. I asked the manager if I could stay until Monday so I could at least sort this mess out. The hotel was booked out for the coming Ramadan festival, he told me, and yelled, 'You must leave! You pay now!' He picked up a chair and started banging the table with its legs. It got scary very quickly.

A taxi driver who hung out at the front of the hotel decided to get involved. He came into the office and started yelling at me. 'You pay, you pay!' The week before, when I had money and used his taxi to get to and from local bars, he was my best mate. We used to talk every day. Before I knew it, there was a crowd around me.

Where the hell did they come from? People started coming from everywhere, like black ninjas out of the cracks in the walls in a cheap kung fu movie.

Then one of the locals said, 'You come with me to the police'. I thought that was a good idea at the time. 'We'll sort it out there', I told them. I was still hopeful that my phone or wallet had been handed in to Kuta Police Station, which was the nearest. I hopped on the back of a motorbike with the local man and we rode off to the police station.

The previous year, the Bali police had moved the office of its 'tourist police' from the headquarters in downtown Denpasar to Kuta, in the heart of the tourist district. The friendly-looking brochure I saw on the front desk there stated: '15 officers working 24 hours a day, who speak fluent English, Japanese, Spanish and Mandarin, are on duty to help tourists on any issue'.

They would help me, right? If I was expecting a friendly face and a quick resolution to my situation, I was sadly mistaken.

I walked in to Kuta Police Station with the group of angry locals from the hotel. Inside, there were six policemen sitting behind a huge desk with their arms folded. I tried to tell them my story but I was quickly interrupted in Indonesian by several of the people from the hotel and everyone started talking at the same time, so I decided to sit down until the police were ready to speak to me.

The police station was several degrees cooler than outside. There was a huge map of Bali on the wall behind the main desk, and behind that wall was an army of detectives sitting at small desks with a long bench running along the back of the room. The police at the front desk wore dark grey uniforms, whereas the detectives who later interviewed me were wearing plain clothes—slacks, short- sleeved shirts and nice shoes.

It was a very busy place, with lots of other tourists waiting to be seen by the detectives. Two Australian women were in there waiting to be seen, complaining that they wanted to be kept there all night until their problem was resolved.

After a while, a large policeman came over, his shirt dripping in perspiration, and started banging the table with a metal ruler. 'Why you no pay your fucking bill?' he yelled. The locals started shouting again and the situation quickly spiralled out of control.

'I will tell you what happened', I told them. 'I will explain it all to you. All I need is to call Australia and I will sort this out and pay my bill. Can I please use a phone?' I was going to call some friends in Australia who could get some money to me quickly so that this nightmare would soon be over.

'No, you don't call no one!' the policeman yelled. My heart sunk as I realised the quick resolution I had been hoping for was not on his agenda.

The hotel manager came to the desk and handed the police my passport, so doing a runner wasn't an option. I wasn't going anywhere. It was getting very angry now and I was beginning to fear for my safety. I asked to see the Australian consulate, feebly demanding my rights. But when the police looked at my passport they saw that I was born in New Zealand and therefore had a Kiwi passport. The Kuta police said I had to talk to the New Zealand consulate.

'I don't want to talk to the New Zealand consulate', I told them. 'I'm Australian!'

The detectives started yelling at me. They took me into another room behind the front counter and plain-clothed policemen started coming in and out. I didn't realise that many detectives were out on the street at any one time.

The detectives contacted the New Zealand consulate anyway. The consulate offered to contact my family as a matter of course, but all my family's numbers were stored in my stolen mobile phone. I didn't know any of their phone numbers off by heart—not even an email address—which speaks volumes of the state my family relationships were in at the time. My father spent most of the year in Thailand now he had retired and he was possibly overseas somewhere. I hadn't talked to my brother in two or three years and I hadn't spoken to mum for eight years. Some time ago, my stepsister had sent me a message on Facebook with some contact information for Mum, but for whatever reason, I hadn't acted on it. I just kept putting it off and putting it off. Years later, I still hadn't contacted them.

But now, sitting in Kuta Police Station, I remembered this piece of information and knew that if I could access Facebook I could at least retrieve my mother's contact details, talk to her and my brother and get the money I needed sent to Bali to sort the whole situation out. For a second I was relieved. I asked the police if I could use their computer to access Facebook. 'No, you pay', was all they said.

Once again, I tried to explain my situation to them. 'I can't pay', I pleaded. 'I have no money. Can I please use your computer? Do you understand?'

'You pay now', they demanded again, pounding on the desk again for effect.

I was losing my patience. 'I don't know what's wrong with you people', I told them. 'I want to pay, so why won't you help me sort this out?'

After almost a full day of arguing, I was still there that night. Sometime during the night, the police put handcuffs on me and chained me to the desk. 'Why the handcuffs?' I asked. Was that really necessary?

'You now a criminal', one of the policemen told me.

At some point during that first long night in Indonesian custody, I was trying to sleep while handcuffed to a wooden desk when a young lady came up and sat beside me.

'Paul?' she asked.

'Yeah?' I mumbled, still half asleep.

Her name was Sara. She was very small, barely five foot tall (152 cm), and quite attractive with makeup on and her hair in a bun. She was dressed professionally. She said she worked for a lawyer in Los Angeles, of all places. She also worked for the police as translator, she said, helping Westerners like me who were in trouble with the local police.

I trusted her straight away. I had no reason not to. I was just grateful to speak to someone, so I never doubted a word she said. She said she was here to help me and I was grateful to finally talk to someone who would listen to me.

'How are you?' she asked.

'Not too good', I told her. 'This is out of control. My wallet and phone have been stolen and I have no access to my money or credit cards'. Showing her my handcuffs I added, 'How the hell did I get here?'

I assumed that Sara had been appointed by the New Zealand consulate to liaise with the police because she spoke fluent English and translated everything I said to the police into Indonesian. I told her everything that had happened and that I needed to get in contact with my father in Sydney or my family in the States, but nobody would give me access to a phone or a computer.

'What is the number?' Sara asked helpfully, pulling out her phone. 'I'll call them for you'. I explained to her that I had all my phone numbers stored in my mobile phone, but I knew that my Mum's number was posted on my Facebook page by my stepsister. Sara didn't have the Internet on her phone so she couldn't access Facebook. She said she would see me the following morning at 10 a.m. and that she would sort it all out.

I was taken upstairs to a holding cell for the night, relieved that someone in this situation seemed to be fighting my corner, and looking forward to the next morning when Sara would come and resolve the problem. But morning came, and with it no sign of Sara.

I ultimately spent 58 days at Kuta Police Station in a small cell with a dozen other prisoners, being dragged back and forth to incomprehensible Indonesian court sessions like a common criminal.

And this was before I even ended up in Bali's Kerobokan Prison. Over the next two months I almost lost my mind.

CHAPTER 2

THE STING

I was born in Auckland, New Zealand, in 1968. Dad was Welsh, and a long way from home, while Mum was Latvian. I don't know how they met. Mum and Dad didn't share many 'courting' tales in the several short years they were together, but I know Dad was in the Air Force at the time and Mum was a nurse. Let's just call it fate!

We moved to Australia when I was about six months old, and having spent no time that I remember in New Zealand, I have always considered myself to be Australian. In 2012, however, the Bali Police and the Australian Federal Government saw it another way.

The Conibeer family settled in Blackheath, in the Blue Mountains west of Sydney, but we moved to Auburn in Sydney's Inner West when Dad went to work at the Blackwoods factory in Smithfield. My brother David was born in Australia in 1970. Our parents split up when I was only two or three years old, but Dad sought custody of my brother and me and he was the one who raised us. Dad was strict, but he didn't smoke or drink and he had a great work ethic, which he endeavoured to pass on to us. We didn't have a lot of money, but somehow Dad held it all together.

I don't know to this day what happened between Mum and Dad and why they split up. Mum took off and lived with a guy called Max in Auburn. They had a child together, my half-sister Kim. Her mum, my grandmother, lived at Bondi and I used to love visiting there on weekends and going to the beach. It was a world away from the Western Suburbs.

I went to school at Auburn South Public School, then St Joseph the Worker Catholic School in the same suburb and later Holroyd High School. I did okay at school considering I hated Maths and loathed English—all those books to read. But I loved sport. I played soccer for Auburn Federation and later Blacktown City, and I met the famous Waugh twins, Steve and Mark. They were a couple of years older than me, as was Robbie Slater, who played for St George juniors and later captained Australia, but I can still remember the day the reps coach said to the Waugh brothers, 'You guys have to make a decision whether you want to play cricket or soccer'.

Steve and Mark Waugh, of course, went on to become two of the greatest post-war cricketers Australia has produced.

I was a pretty good player back then. I won a trip to Yugoslavia to train with the Vojvodina Club for a couple of weeks when I was about 12 years old. I played in front of 40,000 people at one of the games. I had a dream of becoming a professional soccer player, but I was troubled by an Achilles tendon injury as a teenager and soon that dream was over. I had a couple of operations, but the injury never healed and I was never the same player again.

My brother Dave and I saw Mum fairly regularly when she was living in Sydney, but when I was aged 13 she sat us down and told us she was moving to the United States. Her life with Max hadn't worked out and she was heading off to California with an American named Howard, someone a friend had set her up on a date with and the relationship had taken off. I was devastated. Mum was leaving us a second time. It would be another six years before I saw her again.

At school, I went on to Year 11 but I only lasted a couple of days. When the teachers showed me the boxes of books I had to read I said bugger that, and walked home. I lay on the couch until Dad came home and he asked me straight away, 'What do you think you're doing?' I told him I had quit school; I didn't want to go on and do the Higher School Certificate. He told me I was kidding myself if I thought I was going on the dole and sitting around the house all day. I had to get a job, or at the very least, go down to the local college and sign up for a course.

I went over to Granville Technical College that afternoon and signed up for a fitter and machinist pre-apprenticeship course. A neighbour worked for Qantas as a sheet-metal worker. I had always had a fascination for planes and the thought of working on them really appealed to me. Qantas was hiring for the first time in years and ended up putting on five apprentice fitter machinists. More than 500 people applied for the job and I was one of the five selected, as was my neighbour's son—the guy was obviously tight with the people who mattered.

Sydney was a great place to grow up in the 1980s. There was a great party vibe going on for young blokes like me. At any pub in the city, you could catch an up and coming band or enjoy one dollar drinks at 'Sweethearts' at Cabramatta, 'Jacksons' on George Street in the City or catch a train to Cronulla Leagues Club. I don't know how I got home some nights. Some nights I didn't have to. I had no steady girlfriends to speak of and was free to do what I wanted. I worked hard at Qantas in a job I loved. It was a great life.

I completed my full apprenticeship at Qantas, all three years, but I desperately wanted to escape Sydney and go to California where my mother was then living. My father said I wasn't going anywhere until I'd finished my apprenticeship and received my fitter and machinist certificate. With that completed, he told me, I could do anything I wanted and go anywhere in the world. He was right to a certain degree; that course kept me grounded through my teenage years. The same could not be said for my younger brother.

Dave grew into bit of a lad—the wild child of the family—and he was in and out of jail during his teenage years. Nothing too serious: stealing cars and petty burglary—juvenile stuff—after he hooked up with the wrong crowd for a while and suffered the consequences. Perhaps that's why Dad was so tough on me, not wishing to repeat the mistakes he had made in letting Dave get away with things. It's ironic, though, that Dave had the troubled childhood and I was the one who ended up in prison and needed his help.

'What the fuck?' he laughed when I first phoned him and told him I was in jail in Bali. 'I thought you were on the "straight and narrow" and you're in the worse place on earth'. We both laugh about it now, but at the time?

Well, let's just say there wasn't that much to laugh about.

• • •

Sara, my Indonesian interpreter and the only person who had given me any help since I'd been held in Kuta Police Station, seemed to have disappeared. Without her translation I had no idea what was happening when, later on in my second night there, the police came and got me from a holding cell upstairs and shoved a form in front of my face.

'You sign', they said.

'What is this, some sort of charge sheet?' It was all in Indonesian. 'I'm not signing anything', I said stoically.

'You sign!'

The police said the sheet was 'my information', and showed me where my name was printed. I had no one to advise me and I was still waiting to see an official from my consulate, so eventually I signed it. What else could go wrong?

'You must pay 3,000 dollars now,' they said as soon as I had signed the paper.

3,000? What the fuck for?

The 3,000, I was informed, was to cover the hotel bill and a 'fine' from the police chief upstairs. They said, or I thought they said, I had 16 days to pay the fine or I would have to go to court. I balked. Sixteen days? I couldn't stand the thought of one more night in that cell. I needed to get hold of someone on the phone to be able to pay the bill and the bribe, but no one at Kuta Police Station was helping me do that so I wouldn't be able to pay no matter how long they gave me.

As I sat in a downstairs office, stunned at the situation I had found myself in, I spied one of the policemen checking his mobile phone. I asked him whether he had access to the Internet. He did, and I pleaded with him to let me check my Facebook page, just for a minute. Amazingly, after all the trouble I had gone through in the previous 48 hours, he gave me his phone. Although the websites were in Indonesian, somehow I navigated my way through the web until I found my Facebook page. At last I was able to access my brother's phone number and my mother's email address, but couldn't contact my family until Sara came back with her phone. All I could do was wait for her and hope she would come back.

Sara finally reappeared on day three at Kuta Police Station with no explanation as to where she had been the previous two days. I had the numbers ready for her when she sat beside me. She looked at me confused. 'How did you get the numbers?' she asked. I told her a policeman finally let me access his phone and she looked a little amazed. She handed me her phone and I dialled my brother's American phone number.

As the phone rang I thought of the last time we had spoken, years before, and felt a sense of disbelief that I was now calling under these circumstances. Eventually, my brother's voice filled the receiver. It was a little uncomfortable to begin with as I struggled to get my story out, and how and why I now needed his help.

'Dave, I am in real trouble in Bali', I told him. 'I've had my phone and wallet stolen and I am in Kuta Police Station until I pay. Could you get some money to me, quickly?'

Dave said he had no cash to speak of. He could get a small loan against his house to cover about 5,000 dollars, but it would take a couple of days to organise. The problem was, it was already Friday and the Monday was a public holiday in the States so nothing could be done until after the weekend.

'Who will I send the money to?' Dave asked. I had no idea. It was not as if I could walk down to the ATM to collect it. I would have no choice but to send it to Sara. I asked her how Dave could get the money to her in the next 16 days. And that's when I found out that it was not 16 days I had been given—it was six. I only had six days to get the money to her before the matter went to court. And one more thing, she said, the fine was now 5,500 dollars.

'What?! Why has the money gone up again?' I asked. 'Immigration', Sara replied vaguely. 'You must pay immigration to leave the country'. This was all bullshit, I told her. My brother could only get a loan for 5,000 dollars and Sara knew that. I only had six days to pay up and I was losing four days over the long weekend.

There was no way I could make it happen.

I rang Dave again and he said he couldn't get the money I needed until the following Wednesday—the day after the matter had to go to court. Dave didn't know what to do and I could tell he was worried for me. I asked him to contact my friends on Facebook to let them know I was in trouble. Alert the Australian media that I was being extorted, I implored him, thinking the media shock jocks and news services would jump on the issue of another Australian locked up in a Bali prison. Dave contacted everyone, including several media outlets, but no one could come up with the money in time or disappointingly, even wanted to help. Maybe my closest friends weren't my friends after all.

By the time Wednesday rolled around, the amount I had to pay had magically risen to 7,000 dollars. If the matter went to court, I was informed, I would also need to get a good lawyer, which would cost another 5,000 dollars. I was really in a hole. Dave tried to hire an Indonesian lawyer but when he realised I had no money he said he wouldn't be able to extend the deadline anyway and he walked out on me. Sara had not visited in days. I was alone and resigned to spending a long time in the cramped holding cell at Kuta.

Every day, the Kuta police were demanding, 'You must pay money to get released'. 'Now you must pay more money because you miss the expiry date'. 'You must pay immigration'. My head was spinning.

I was holding out hope that when someone from the New Zealand consulate eventually came to visit me they would see the plight I was in and help me. This was not to be the case. When the consular official finally arrived at Kuta Police Station I tried desperately to explain to him that I was being set up. The police were trying to frame me and extort money from me, I told him. The problem remained that the police sergeant was sitting right beside me when the consular official was in the room. I really needed to speak to him alone—in private. I even asked the police chief if I could speak privately to my consulate and he just sat there with his arms crossed.

'See', I told the consular official, 'this is what I am trying to tell you!' I was getting nowhere.

The consular official said that if I wanted to talk to him privately I could call him, but of course I didn't have access to a phone. It was as if he hadn't listened to a word I had said. I just looked at him. 'This is fucked', I told him. 'No one cares. No one gives a flying fuck. What's going to happen to me?'

'The best thing you can do', the official said, 'is to get a lawyer'. 'I can't afford a lawyer!' I told him. 'I have no money and no credit cards, remember? That's why I am in this trouble, remember?'

I asked if he could employ a lawyer for me, and he said that the New Zealand government didn't do that. Then he hit me with this priceless advice: 'Paul', he said, 'Learn to adapt to your situation!' Learn to adapt? Was he serious?

'Why would you waste your time flying down from Jakarta to tell me that piece of wisdom?' I said. Thanks a lot.

The following day Sara came back to the police station.

Increasingly desperate, I again phoned Dave using her phone. He told me he had discussed the issue with Mum and they would do anything they could to help me. Mum could apply for a house loan of 20,000 dollars but it was going to take 30 days to come. He said he would hop on a plane as soon as he got the money through.

Telling Sara this was a big mistake. I should have kept it to myself, but at this point I had little choice but to trust Sara and I hoped that she would still help me. As soon as I told her my mother and brother could secure a loan for 20,000 dollars, the price for my release went up to 16,000 dollars.

After a week in Kuta Police Station, all I wanted to do was to get out of Bali. And I was prepared to pay the 16,000 dollars if that meant I would be released and deported straight away. I had assumed that if I paid the fine I would be able to leave, but when I asked Sara if this was how it worked, all she said was 'We'll see'.

'We'll see? The answer is either yes or no', I thought. There was no 'we'll see' as far as I was concerned. 'It is up to the police', Sara said, and she wouldn't give me a firm answer. But it was still going to take 30 days to get the money to her anyway. I had no control over that.

After a couple of weeks, Dave was able to wire me a couple of hundred dollars. I gave 50 dollars to Sara, with a promise that the bigger amount would arrive soon and this ordeal would all be over. I had about 150 dollars, or about 2 million rupiah, to buy some toiletries and food. Finally, Sara admitted that even if I paid the 16,000 dollars I would probably still go to jail as the matter had to go to court because we had passed the expiry date. If she had got the money before the date, she said, she could have paid the police off. Not now. I was desperate to have this resolved, and the thought of going to prison in Bali filled me with a sense of dread. Kerobokan, the home of the Bali Nine and Schapelle Corby, had a terrible reputation and I didn't know how long I could last in the cell upstairs in the police station.

It was clear the Kuta police were trying to extort money out of me to stop my case from going to court. They obviously didn't want the matter to come before the international media, who were all over the island after the arrest of Schapelle Corby, the Bali Nine and more recently, British grandmother Lindsay Sandiford. Worst of all it seemed that Sara, my interpreter and police-appointed court liaison, was part of the extortion.

My brother Dave is a pretty cut and dried sort of guy. When I told him what was going on he said, bluntly, to tell the police to go fuck themselves. 'Dave', I pleaded, 'That's easy for you to say, but I need to get out of here'. Dave said he could smell a rat. 'Just pay the money, Dave', I said. 'I just want to go home'.

That night, I went back to my cell and I thought about my situation all through the night. I didn't even know how I was going to get the 16,000 dollars to Sara. Is Dave supposed to wire it? Should he bring it over himself on a plane? Who do I give it to? The next day I asked Sara whether Dave could send the money to me in my name and I could go to collect it. 'The Police can take me down to Western Union', I said.

Sara shook her head and said to wire it to the police station in *her* name, and that she would ensure it got to the people who mattered.

Now I smelt the same rat that Dave did. I knew that there was a 10 per cent surcharge on the wiring of money through Western Union, so my 16,000 dollars would effectively only total 14,400 dollars after the fee. There was no way in the world that the police going were going to let me get away with paying them 1,600 dollars less than they had asked for and still let me leave. The cold reality of my situation had finally set in. The police were going to keep all the money and still send me to jail.

The following day, Sara met me downstairs in the police station and asked when the money was arriving. Trying to stall for time and find out more about my real situation, I told her it was coming soon. I still didn't even know what I was being charged with.

There was a large whiteboard with the names of all the prisoners in the cell written on it in rows. I had recognised my name on the whiteboard with the number '378' beside it. An Indonesian security guard named Ronald, who was in the Kuta cell with me after being charged with fighting, told me that number was my charge number. 'What does it mean?' I asked him. 'Fraud and deception', Ronald said. The police were charging me with trying to scam the hotel. But, hang on! I was the victim!

'It could be worse', Ronald said. 'Could be 121'. 'What does 121 stand for?' I enquired *Narkoba* … narcotics, drugs.

A drug charge is every jailed Westerner's worst nightmare.

Indonesia is famous for its strict drug laws and even possessing a small amount can land you with a jail sentence of up to 12 years, not to mention the death penalty for smugglers of hard drugs like the Bali Nine ringleaders received. Indonesian parents can even be jailed for failing to inform authorities of their own children's drug use. These laws have not done much to curb the drug problem in Indonesia, and in Bali drug dealers roam the streets relatively freely thanks to the bribes they pay the police. It's common to be offered drugs in Bali, and for those who are caught buying or selling the effects can be devastating.

When I went to Denpasar District Court for the first time, I saw Sara talking to the police chief and a prosecutor. Afterwards, she came over to me and said I also had to pay the prosecutor 5,500 dollars so he would reduce the charge. If not, she said, I would get the full term—seven years. By this point I had little faith in anything Sara had to say, so I decided to wait until I had spoken to Dave before I would make any decisions.

After my court appearance—during which my case was adjourned to a future date—Sara let me use her phone to call my brother. I turned away from her and I discreetly asked Dave to Google '378' in Indonesian law and see what the maximum sentence was. Dave looked it up as we spoke and told me there was another case of an Australian guy who cheated someone out of 250,000 dollars by selling some land that wasn't his and all he got was four years.

'Mate', Dave said. 'If you stole 1,200 dollars, you wouldn't even get that much time in jail. And this woman is telling you you'll get seven years? Tell her to fuck off! They're only trying to squeeze some money out of you'. Dave even offered to come over to Bali and pay the hotel bill himself but it was too late for that. The date for any compromise had expired and my case was going to be heard in front of a judge anyway.

After ten days sleeping on the floor of a cell in Kuta Police Station it finally dawned on me. Dave was right. Fuck the police. Fuck the Indonesian justice system. I was not going to play their game anymore.

I confronted Sara about what I knew about the fraud and deception charges. 'When I spoke to my brother, he said the maximum sentence was four years', I told her. The expression on her face changed straight away. 'How do you know the sentence is only four years?' she asked.

'My brother looked it up on the Internet', I said. 'It's Indonesian law'. I was really angry now.

When we sat down with the prosecutor, I asked him whether Sara and the police chief had come to see him about my case. He said he had spoken to the police chief but he had never spoken to Sara about me. 'She's telling me I have to give you 5,500 dollars or you'll give me seven years in prison', I said. He looked confused and reiterated that he had never talked to Sara about my case.

I made up my mind. 'I'm sorry to say this to you', I told Sara, 'but you're full of shit'. I called her a liar in front of the police and her demeanour changed straight away. She started talking to the police in Indonesian so I spoke directly to them.

'Tell her to get out of my sight and I'll take my chances in court'. Sara was horrified. She had made out she was on my side, interpreted for the police and claimed she was going to help me, but all the while she was trying to extort money from me. My mother and brother were calling Sara directly on her phone but as soon as I told her I wasn't going to pay any of the money she cut off all contact with them. I never saw her again after that day. Because of this I had no way of communicating with anyone in the outside world. I didn't hear from my brother again for three weeks and by that time I was in Kerobokan Prison. He had no idea what was happening to me.

CHAPTER 3

MY DAY IN COURT

Kuta Police Station was a hellhole. I was the only *bule* (Western male) crammed in a cell with a dozen other inmates. In another cell, several women waited their turn to go to court. The cell was about 8 feet (2.4m) wide by 10 feet (3.1m) long; I am 6 foot tall and when I lay down on the tiled floor I could touch the walls with my feet and the wall behind me with my hands.

The toilet was in a corner of the cell behind a wooden door.

There were walls on three sides of the cell, with bars on the fourth wall acting as a window to the outside. The prisoners washed their underpants and singlets in the bathroom and draped them over a ledge on top of one of the walls or across the bars, blocking the only air into the cell, so they could dry.

The Kuta police often came upstairs to take photos of me. I was big news for them—another Aussie in a Bali jail—but not a soul back home knew where I was or what had happened to me.

The police at Kuta did head counts every two hours after three escapes in the previous six months. In September 2011, six men were being held on drugs and fraud charges when they broke through the wall of the toilet adjoining their holding cell on the fourth floor of the police station at about one o'clock in the morning. Somehow, the detainees accessed the tools needed to make the hole in the wall, as well as the rope they used to lower themselves to the ground, and appeared to have planned the breakout thoroughly.

They risked broken bones in jumping from the fourth floor before fleeing through a construction site behind the police station. That's how desperate they were to get out of there. Five of the men were later recaptured. The following week an Indonesian man escaped by breaking through the floor of his cell into the room below. In February 2012, a young boy managed to escape after he noticed the lock on his cell was broken.

The police didn't update the names of the prisoners on the whiteboard, and we would remind them that certain prisoners had left for Kerobokan or had be freed. They would be calling names of people who had left weeks before. 'He's not here, mate', I would tell them. 'He's already gone'. They had no idea. When workmen were fixing the roof of the police station and had been hammering away for three days, several police rushed in with guns drawn thinking we were trying to escape.

The police were incompetent. They couldn't open the door to our cell one day. They called a colleague over to help them and he just stared at it. An Indonesian prisoner inside the cell actually reached through the bars and jiggled the key until it opened. It was hilarious.

The police were so bored they stole our playing cards and we caught them playing with them. Yet, there was always the fear that something random would happen. At night, the guards kept saying 'go to sleep'. Not only was it too uncomfortable to sleep, but I was worried about what would happen to me if I did.

Our cell was on the fourth floor of the police station. There was no elevator, only stairs, so the lazy, fat policemen had to carry the prisoners' water from the ground floor to the fourth floor. We got one bottle a day—half a litre of water—and it was so hot. There were no windows, no fans and we couldn't see the sky. It was just dark and humid. There was no smoking allowed, but incredibly people would still smoke in the confined spaces of the cell. If we were caught smoking, the police would come to the cell, grab a prisoner and smash him in the guts. The police used to smoke cigarettes in front of us. They'd sit there and smoke with a grin on their faces, but if we got caught smoking, look out.

We were fed at seven o'clock in the morning and six at night, mainly rice with a huge wad of chilli in it and the smallest piece of egg, with two long green beans and a piece of chicken. I have no idea where anatomically the piece of chicken came from but it tasted like the arse. By the time I took the fat and gristle off it there was a piece of meat left the size of my fingernail. I ate it quickly because I was so hungry. If grains of rice fell on the floor I picked them up and ate them too, no matter whose meal they came from. I would wait for people to get up off the floor after they ate and I would eat what was left behind. That's how desperate I was.

While I was there, the manager from the hotel came to the police station and tried to charge me with a string of frauds. There were a few hotels in the area where people had not paid their bills, and they decided to charge me with the lot. Several hotel owners turned up to my cell and they just pointed me out. 'Paul?' the police would call out. 'What?' I'd reply. They then just looked at me and nodded their heads and walked off. What was all that about? Later, the police brought in another hotel owner. 'Paul, this guy wants to talk to you', they said. 'Who is he?' I asked.

'Just look over at him', they said. I didn't even know who he was, but I gave him a wave and he walked off.

The police told me they had amassed quite a collection of unpaid bills from all of my supposed crimes, and were keeping them in a large, folding file. I called it the 'Penski file', from the famous Seinfeld episode, because it was so laughable.

'Look how thick your file is', the police would taunt.

'Pretty thick for one hotel account, mate', I'd shoot back. But I needed to see that file.

The New Zealand consulate tried to get hold of Dad, but they couldn't contact him. They later tried several other people I knew back in Australia, but no one could help me or wanted to help me. If I waited five or six weeks, a few friends said, they might be able to get some money to me. Five or six weeks? Today, various friends have said that I should have called them for help, but I didn't think I had a good enough relationship with them to ask them to bail me out. Pride is a funny thing.

During my time at the police station, the words the New Zealand consulate told me—'Learn how to adapt'—kept ringing in my ears.

I rang the consulate weeks later when I was about to go

back to court without a lawyer. The consular official replied that there was nothing he could do for me. 'That's all right', I told him, 'You've done nothing for me anyway. I haven't heard from you in weeks'. His reply? Another pearl of wisdom: 'Well, I didn't have anything to tell you'.

The New Zealand consulate later sent me an official fax, stating they could not interfere with Indonesian law, nor could they assist me financially. 'Try and learn the language while you're there so you can understand what is going on', they suggested. Genius. Their advice wasn't worth the cheap fax paper it was printed on.

In the 58 days I spent at Kuta Police Station I had no visitors. There was a long hallway leading from the cell, and if I got the angle right, I could see people waiting to visit. There was a young

Indonesian guy in my cell who had been arrested for fighting in a nightclub (he later got six months). He was looking up the hallway one morning and started calling out to me. 'Paul, Paul... *bule, bule*'. 'What?' I asked. I had a look up the hallway to see a white girl waiting in the hallway. Maybe someone knows about me? I started to think. Maybe someone has heard about my case? I was the only white person there, right? Perhaps she was there to see me?

She wasn't. I never even spoke to her.

Once a day we were all allowed outside for some exercise. We were supposed to get 15 minutes every day at eleven o'clock. I counted 11 days where we didn't get out of the cells and had no exercise. My body was killing me. I needed to get outside to walk around; you can't walk around in a circle in a cell for 58 days and stay sane. Honestly, if I had to spend another day in there I would have completely lost my mind.

After lying on a concrete tiled floor for almost two months I swear it became softer. It really did. I used a water bottle for a pillow. It was all I had. Someone left and I grabbed a towel from them—a dirty old towel I hung on to for dear life. Another prisoner named John got me toothpaste and a brush; his wife bought them for me.

I had to be resourceful and I pulled it all together from absolutely nothing. I showered twice a day, morning and at night, just to stay clean in the humid conditions.

I went to Denpasar District Court nine times before I received my final sentence, and by that time I had already been shifted to Kerobokan Prison. Kuta Police Station only had a small holding cell and the station only dealt with minor crimes. The drug dealers and murderers were all held at the bigger Polda Police Station.

The second time I went to court the judge asked, 'Where's your lawyer?' I didn't have one so I decided to defend myself. I didn't understand a word the court said for eight weeks. After I got rid of Sara I was assisted by an interpreter who told me I needed to get a lawyer. 'The judge won't talk to you without a lawyer', she said. Sometimes I would go to court and sit there all day, only to have my case adjourned. Other times, I would be in court for only a couple of minutes and the judge would say, 'you come back next week'.

It was extremely frustrating, but because I didn't have a lawyer I didn't know if and when I needed to be in court. I had no one to advise me. When I went to court, I would ask my interpreter if it was my turn to speak. 'Just wait, just wait', she'd say. I didn't know what was going on. On one occasion, I recognised the manager from my hotel who lodged the original complaint, but he was standing with a group of Indonesian businessmen, including some of the guys who had come to visit me in my cell. Something was going on.

The judge finally showed me the file of papers the police had on me. 'Is this your signature?' he asked, pointing at the hotel account from where I had stayed. 'Yes, it is', I replied. 'Is this?' he said, fishing out another. 'No, it's not. It's a forgery', 'Is this?' he said again. "No, another forgery.' I couldn't believe it.

I needed to look at the paperwork they had on me. One day in court, the prosecutor brought the file over to the desk and finally showed me. My hotel account from where I had stayed was dated and signed by me, but they weren't my signatures on the other hotel accounts, nor was I there on those dates. I couldn't have been, I told my interpreter. How could I stay in four hotels at the same time?

Someone was setting me up.

I began to resign myself to going to Kerobokan. In the end, I had become tired of explaining myself and I just kept telling the police to send me to prison. I was so frustrated. I couldn't communicate with them. They were so docile, so vacant; I felt like smacking a wall to get my story told. It got to the point where I asked myself, 'Is this a dream? How did I end up here? I couldn't be that stupid'. As much as I wanted to tell the police to go fuck themselves, I was trying to hold it all together.

One day in court the manager of the hotel approached me to see if we could come to some agreement. He wanted his money. 'Listen',

I told him. 'I tried to sort this out; I tried to get you your money but Sara stuffed everything up and here I am. So, if you want your money, go talk to her'.

For me, my Kuta 'experience', awful as it was, was ultimately a positive one because it prepared me for Kerobokan. It hardened me for what lay ahead. I would have hated to do the sentence in reverse, finishing my time in Kerobokan and then doing 58 days at Kuta.

Throughout the whole experience, Dave's words, 'tell 'em to get fucked', rang in my head. I thought that was a pretty ballsy mentality, so I just decided to adopt his attitude.

I wasn't going to play their game. Perhaps I just didn't care anymore.

The police could only hold me at Kuta Station for 60 days, so as I approached that mark I knew I was going to be moved to Kerobokan before my sentencing. Ronny, the Indonesian guy I befriended in Kuta Police Station, had told me all about 'Hotel K'. 'Don't do drugs; don't borrow money and you'll be fine', he said. 'No one will touch you. You are a big *bule*'. I hoped he was right.

As the days went on I started watching other people leave for Kerobokan and I realised they were actually being taken two or three days before their 60 days were up. So by day 58, I knew I would be next. I was lying on the floor of the cell when, at ten o'clock on the dot, the door to the cell opened and I knew it was time to leave. The police had the handcuffs ready and I could hear them rattling before they even reached the door. Everyone in the cell with me knew I was leaving. As I walked down the corridor away from the cell, handcuffed and flanked by two officers, I actually felt relieved to be leaving, even if it was to go to one of the most infamous prisons in the world.

I was taken out of Kuta Police Station and led into the back of a white police van handcuffed to another prisoner.

CHAPTER 3

I had the biggest smile on my face as I left the station, but I knew my happiness would only be momentary. The windows of the bus were down and the wind blew in my face. I leaned out of the window, enjoying the sun.

The police took us to the courthouse and put me in a holding cell for the day. I had no idea what was happening. After court finished at 4 p.m., prisoners to be transferred and prisoners facing sentencing were taken to another police van.

One of the policemen told me I was going to be taken to Polda Police Station for thirty days, which really filled me with dread. Another police station? I didn't want to go to any other prison in Bali where I would be locked away and forgotten. Then they confirmed I was going to Kerobokan.

The heat inside was stifling. My mouth was dry but I was happy to be leaving Kuta and not heading to another police station.

While on the bus I met Lindsay Sandiford for the first time. She was waiting to be sentenced for drug trafficking; I had read about her situation in a newspaper in Kuta Police Station. She was handcuffed to a Ugandan, the blackest man I had ever seen. His name was Bashir, but I later got to know him inside Kerobokan and I nicknamed him Black Basil.

The journey from central Kuta to the prison was quick and as we stopped outside the prison I heard the guards shouting to each other and the police, probably discussing the new arrivals. The door to the van opened and I took my first steps into Kerobokan Prison.

CHAPTER 4

'HOTEL K'

There was a really cool dude who I looked up to at Qantas—an original hippie with long hair and beard—who first told me about Bali when I was a teenaged apprentice in the late 1980s. 'You have to go there', he said. 'It's the greatest place on earth... you party, drink piss and there's heaps of chicks'.

Really? I had never heard of the place. Bali? When I got there I thought it was out of this world.

Working at Qantas, we were able to buy cheap flights to Bali whenever we wanted them. It cost us about 55 dollars a flight, and because we worked for the company we could check if the flight was full the week before departure and secure a seat. A group of us would finish work at two o'clock in the afternoon and catch the afternoon flight to Bali at 4.30 p.m. After hopping on a shuttle bus to the international airport with the stewardesses on our flight, we'd hit the bar straight away. We'd arrive in Bali at midnight and head straight to the nightclubs.

We'd always stay at a place called the Bukensari Cottages, which we quickly renamed the 'Fuckin' Sorry' Cottages. Accommodation was 7 dollars a night—just 14 dollars for the weekend—at a time when you could drink all night on 20 dollars.

The problem was that the plane for the return trip to Australia left at midnight on Sunday and it landed just before we had to start work at 7 a.m. on Monday. We'd step straight off the plane and catch the minibus to the other side of the terminal, put our overalls on and start work. When I was a young bloke, I could stay on the drink all day, fly home through the night and start work the next morning. We'd be blind drunk at Denpasar Airport, crashed out on the airport lounges like shattered sharks, and the Indonesian airport staff would stare at us in disbelief.

As soon as I finished my apprenticeship at age 19 in 1988, I flew to America to reunite with my mother. Dad and I were not getting along at all; Dave was in trouble again and Dad was taking it out on me. I didn't need the aggravation anymore and when my grandmother offered to pay for my flight I jumped at the chance. I wanted to get to know my mother better because I hadn't seen her for several years, and I went to live with her in California where she was working as a nurse.

I loved America. 'Crocodile Dundee' had just been released and as soon as I opened my mouth I was treated like a movie star. Thank you, Paul Hogan. I actually met 'Hoges' on the flight to America—he was heading off to make 'Crocodile Dundee II', but I had no idea of the impact he had made on the States until I got there. I had nothing for Hoges to write on when I asked him for an autograph, so I got him to sign an in- flight magazine. The picture? A crocodile, of course.

Living in America in the late 1980s, it was as if I only had to speak and the local girls were interested. I'd go to a bar and ask for a Fosters beer, which was the drink of choice at the time, and once they realised I was Australian they would flock around. 'Talk to us', they would say. 'Just say something, anything'. I didn't even have to buy them a drink. It was almost as easy as saying 'Hi' and 'Bye'.

I got some work with a local man who was making circuit boards for the military in an industrial unit, but when he lost the contract I was out of a job. I was trying to get a position at McDonnell Douglas or Boeing

Sentenced to ten months in Kerobokan Prison in 2012.
No one knew who I was or where I was from.

خيركم من تعلم القرآن
3
2

Opposite: A common area in one of the prison blocks. Note the mustard yellow that the entire prison seemed to be painted in and the ubiquitous ping pong table, beside which I slept in Block B.

Left: Inmates preparing a meal and washing up ready for dinner. We cooked our own food as often as possible because the prison food was inedible.

Below: An improvised clothesline at the back of our block. You had to watch your clothes, or pay one of the Indonesian inmates to watch them, otherwise the gangs would steal your belongings.

Opposite: Freeze-dried meals given to our block by one of the visitors. Just add hot water (if you could find a working kettle).

Left: A makeshift power point, made out of a plastic bottle and spare wires, charging one of our contraband phones. It was rudimentary, but it worked.

Below: A snake that got too close to one of the blocks. The meat ended up in a stew we cooked.

BACK COUNTRY
Cuisine

Left: Condiment cabinet, Block B. You could buy some items from the prison canteen, but other things had to be sourced from outside and brought in by visitors.

Below: Our makeshift 'gym': concrete weights set in plastic flowerpots and held together by a scrap metal pole. Every block had its own gym and keeping fit kept us focused in prison because there was just so little to do during the day.

Left: Our evening meal being cooked on the stove in our 'kitchen' at the back of Block B. It's supposed to be pasta.

Below left: Makeshift knives made out of tools used in our block. Not surprisingly, Kerobokan did not supply knives and forks for us to eat with.

Below right: 'There are no weapons in Kerobokan', the prison trumpeted to the media. The problem was that tools like the one I am holding here could also be used as weapons.

The gardens in Kerobokan Prison have been described as like those in a 'down-market resort'. This water feature at the back of our prison block would not win an award, but we used to take advantage of the bench area behind it to dry our clothes or mattresses or lay in the sun. The block immediately behind it is C1, run by the Indonesian gangs.

at the time, but it was just too hard to get a green card. I never did get one, and I worked and lived there for 10 years, paid taxes and earned a good living, all on a false social security number. The number I obtained originally had 'not valid for employment' marked on it, but I needed a social security number to open a bank account so a girl I knew scratched the words off with a pin and it looked real enough to open the account.

One night, I met a little Indian-looking guy in a bar who spoke with a broad English accent. He was playing pool and I challenged him to a game. 'Where are you from?' he asked. 'Where the fuck are you from?' I replied. 'What accent do you call that?'

His name was Bruce Gajjav and he became my best friend in the States. Bruce had just got a job at a Jeep dealership and he asked me if I had ever sold cars? I couldn't do that, I told him, but he said my Australian accent would sell the cars for me. 'The American public are fascinated by Australians and they'll love you', he said. He showed me how much money he was making a month and I couldn't believe it. He was driving a BMW and living the high life, so that was enough for me.

I worked at a Jeep dealership in California for almost 10 years. We were close to the beach and Wranglers sold like hot cakes in the 1990s. All the young, attractive women wanted to drive a Wrangler and as soon as I opened my mouth, I had them hooked. Sometimes, I even had to ask whether they still wanted to buy a car or just hear me talk. It was funny, though. All the salespeople in the dealership were migrants: Bruce, Phil from England, Vince from Lebanon, another guy from Trinidad and me.

I even got Dave a job there when he too came over to the States to reconnect with Mum and get away from trouble back in Sydney.

• • •

Lembaga Permasyarajatan Kerobokan, LP Kerobokan for short or 'Hotel K' to the inmates, Kerobokan is actually the name of the suburb, next to the tourist district of Seminyak, where the prison is situated. Kerobokan was built in 1976 to hold just over 300 inmates, but housed more than three times that number when I arrived there in October 2012. The prison's fading whitewashed walls did not have armed guards outside it, manned towers or surveillance cameras, which would be mandatory in any Western prison.

I wondered what stopped inmates from trying to escape. There were three internal walls before you reached the large external wall. But you wouldn't need to scale them to escape. They were so badly bult you could have charged right through them, Hulk-style.

It wasn't the stories of snakes in long grass and a moat of water around the perimeter that deterred you. I later discovered that the fear of what the guards would do to you if they caught you escaping was enough to keep the 1000 inmates in check.

The walls didn't talk, but somehow they housed the truth.

Dozens of foreigners calling Hotel K home is very good for business, with family and friends, the world's media and the ever- curious tourist making the 30-minute trip from Bali airport to visit the more famous of the inmates. When I arrived there, however, there was no fanfare or media attention. No one knew who I was or what my story was.

There have been a number of riots at the jail in recent years. In February 2012, six months before I arrived, a riot inside the prison started after the stabbing of one prisoner and the arrests of three inmates who were members of Indonesian crime gangs. The riot broke out about 11 p.m. one night, with prisoners trashing cells and attacking the guards who were forced to abandon the overcrowded jail. No prisoners escaped but some inmates gained access to the registration wing of the jail, within sight of the front entrance to the prison, and burned down the front office administration block. Several prisoners were taken to hospital after riot police shot them in the leg with rubber bullets. Guards were beaten back to the streets by rocks and other improvised weapons wielded by rampaging inmates. Early the following morning about 100 heavily armed police entered the jail to quell the riot. After I arrived at Kerobokan I was shown evidence of empty shell cases and spare bullets kept as souvenirs by prisoners that showed police had used live shells to quell the riot. Some of the Westerners confronted the prison guards after the riot and showed them the bullets they had found. This place was to become my home.

I kept hitting a brick wall with the Indonesian justice system and by the time I arrived at Kerobokan I was exhausted mentally, physically and emotionally. I had almost given up because I wasn't being treated fairly. In Indonesia, cash is king and bribery is rife. To put it in perspective the country is currently ranked as more corrupt than India, Thailand and drug hot-spot Columbia. You can get almost anything you need as long as you are willing to pay for it; you can even get away with murder or buy your way out of going to jail. It has often been said that prisons are a reflection of the state of the society they serve, and Kerobokan was a great reflection of the real value of life in Bali.

With its modest green gardens, Hindu temple and tennis court, 'Hotel K' resembles a low-budget hotel. Like any hotel, you could pay for a room 'upgrade' if you had the money. Hell, in Kerobokan, you could even buy a night outside the prison if you bribed the right people. One prisoner famously paid 40,000 dollars so he could spend every night outside the prison with his Balinese wife during his year in custody.

Other prisoners paid the guards to walk out the front gates each morning before coming back at the end of the day to be locked in the rooms at 6 p.m.

I soon realised that this wasn't your ordinary jail. Kerobokan is one of the only jails in the world where the prisoners are in control.

There, prisoners pay for everything: rent, food, simple cooking materials, cleaning products, toiletries and luxuries such as DVD players, iPhones and TVs. Prisoners can even pay for hookers to come in, with the prison guard acting as middle man or pimp. A hooker can be hired for 800,000 rupiah (about 100 dollars), with guards even bringing in a selection of photos for the prisoner to choose from. Unfortunately for him, one prisoner was found having sex with a hooker in the chief prison guard's office and he was thrown in an isolation cell until he could pay his way out.

At Kerobokan, the front reception area was gutted after the riot of the previous February, and I was greeted by charred walls and the smell of smoke. Everything was burnt. There were about 20 of us being processed and they searched my bags, my shoes, everything.

The guards took off our handcuffs and led us through a narrow, turnstile-like barrier into another room.

The guards were matter of fact and businesslike, not giving away any sense of emotion. There was an Indonesian national—a big, mean-looking guy—sitting there with the guards watching everything as it happened. I later found out he was the gang boss in Block A and he was checking out the new inmates. The reception room opened up into an octagonal shaped common area with red tiles on the floor. This was the visitors' area at the time, because the administration area had recently burned down.

There was a huge industrial fan in there and I instinctively positioned myself in front of it because it was so fucking hot. I looked through the bars and across a green courtyard and I could see a building with a large tower. Two young men were sitting out the front of the block and they yelled out to me.

I recognised them straight away as two members of the Bali Nine, Myu Sukumaran and Matthew Norman. Ronald, the Indonesian I met in Kuta Police Station jail, had told them about me.

'There's an Aussie coming', he had told them. 'A big *bule*'. I don't think they believed Ronald because there had been no media about my case. In Kerobokan, inmates generally know who is coming into the prison because it has already been on the news. Drug runners busted at the airport are big news in Bali. The inmates, especially the Westerners, see it on TVs in their cells and then Google the story on contraband smart-phones or secreted laptops. They usually know the whole story before the new arrival comes in.

'What are you in here for?' Myu asked. 'A problem with a hotel bill', I started to explain. 'You're kidding', they both said. I couldn't believe it myself.

There are about a dozen blocks of cells in Kerobokan: Blocks A, B, C1, C2, D, E, F, G, H, J, K and W, the women's wing. On my first day, the prison guards placed all the new inmates into Block J, telling us that we would be there for about a month. A prisoner, not a guard as I was expecting, told us to sit down in the common area and he told us all the rules of the prison. I think his name was Hector, but I didn't understand him too well. He said I had to pay 15,000 rupiah (about $1.50) a month 'rent', even though I slept outside in the common room on the floor. Some prisoners paid 100,000 rupiah because they actually lived and slept in rooms adjoining the common area. I had a little bit of money left from the original 150 dollars Dave had sent to me in Kuta jail, so at least I had my 'rent' covered.

Block J was a rectangular shaped building. The common area was just a long hallway with six rooms situated off three walls. The rooms were very small and there were nine people to a room. The boss extracted a 'donation' from me to stay in Block J: 150,000 rupiah (about 15 dollars). They gave me a bowl of hot noodles and a warm cup of tea and six cigarettes. I just wolfed the food down. I was so hungry and I hadn't eaten hot food for two months. I was dying for a cold can of coke, but they said I could buy one at the canteen the following morning. It was the first thing I did when the canteen opened.

The guards locked the doors to the block at 6 p.m. and then came back at 8 p.m. for the final headcount. They were back the next morning, unlocking the doors at 6 a.m. so that breakfast could be 'served'—a scoop of rice out of a plastic bucket, five pieces of bread and a piece of fruit—and to conduct the first of four head counts for the day.

Block J was packed so full that there was no room to lie down. I managed to find a spot on the concrete floor in the common area and sit down with my back against the wall—this is how I slept during my first night, sitting on the floor without a pillow or blanket. I was the only Westerner in the block and couldn't understand the shouts and conversations going on around me. All of a sudden there was a huge commotion. The noise came first: the sound of people running and a surge of human bodies towards their intended target. I watched as a guy was punched in the face and others jumped on top of him. In another room, a group of gang members were dumping a guy in a bath, time and time again, trying to scare a drug debt out of him.

Later on in the night a big guy charged into the room holding a pair of scissors. He made a beeline for the room closest to where I was sitting and I thought he was going to stab someone. A dozen other guys crowded into the room and I couldn't look. I closed my eyes. No, no, no, dear God no... but they didn't kill him. It turns out they were only trying to cut off his dreadlocks. The Indonesians all piled on top of the poor guy and gave him a haircut. His hair was his prized possession and losing his dreadlocks was punishment for some misdemeanour.

I don't think I had any sleep on my first night in Kerobokan. I may have dozed on and off, but I kept one eye open just in case. It was uncomfortable on the hard floor and hot in the humid conditions. I didn't know a soul inside and I felt wary of everyone.

On the second night, to my amazement, once the guards left us after the eight o'clock head count the inmates in Block J threw a big party—gambling, card games, drinking alcohol, smoking drugs, music—it was an amazing turnaround from the tension of the night before. I was able to mix with the inmates and, in broken English, even 'talked' to a couple of them about my background and how I ended up in prison. There weren't any Westerners in Block J so I wanted to be transferred to another block as soon as possible.

I later learned that I didn't have to worry too much about my safety. The Indonesian gangs wouldn't kill a *bule* in Kerobokan. They could get into a fight with you, whack you over the head with a stick or even stab you with a shank, but they wouldn't kill you. It's an unwritten law. It was heartening to know my government wouldn't have stood for it given all the financial, humanitarian and military aid we give Indonesia each year.

The female prisoners are housed in a separate section of the prison, behind a large steel doorway, 25 metres across from the tennis court. The women in prison are treated as second-class citizens —as they are in Indonesian society— and they don't nearly have the freedom of the male prisoners. Built to house 50 inmates, it currently has more than double that number.

One of the Ugandans named Robert took me to see the prison governor. I walked back through the main gate to the governor's office and I noticed Schapelle Corby and her sister Mercedes sitting on the ground in the visitors' room. I didn't acknowledge them because I was following Robert into the office to sort out where

I was going to stay. Standing in the office in front of the prison governor, I saw a clear plastic tub crammed full of mobile phones. The prison confiscated all phones on the arrival of the inmates, but I later learned they were just as easy to buy inside the prison and the police guards actually sold prisoners phone credit.

'This is Paul', Robert said to the prison governor. 'He wants to move into our block. Is it OK?' The governor was leaning back in his chair, taking it easy as Robert told him my story, and then he leaned forward and said yes straight away. No problem. I could change to Block B, but I had to pay 500,000 rupiah, about 50 dollars, to move blocks. He said they'd give me time to pay.

Schapelle and Mercedes were still there in the visitors' room when I left the prison governor's office. They looked up at me as if to try and work who I was, but I didn't think it was the appropriate time to stop and say hello to them. I was sitting outside the administration office some time later waiting for some paperwork to be processed and the women had to walk past to return to their block. The most infamous of Kerobokan's prisoners spoke to me as she walked past.

Schapelle asked where I was from and I told her I was from Sydney. She asked why I was in Kerobokan and I said I had a problem and I couldn't pay my hotel bill.

'You don't have to worry about this hotel', she remarked. 'It's free'.

I didn't see her again until Christmas. She was so petite and quietly spoken, but she had lovely blue eyes and an enigmatic smile. When I spoke to Schapelle at the Christmas party four months later, she was like an empty vessel. She was a thousand miles away.

The gang boss who was the head of the block did nothing but collect money. The Indonesian prison gangs put him there to shake down the inmates at every opportunity. There were also some Indonesian nationals in Block B because if they went anywhere else they would get killed. There were child molesters, murderers and drug addicts... the cream of the crop.

Block B had an octagonal common area with rooms feeding off every side except for the main entrance, which was locked every night. There were 14 rooms attached to the common area. Each room housed two or three people, with another 20 sleeping on the floor. I was allocated to the Nigerians' room at first. When the prison guards did a roll call and counted heads, I was assigned to that room. There wasn't enough room for three people in there—I only showered in there and dressed—so I slept outside on the floor beside a large ping pong table.

The hard concrete floor was a world away from where I thought I would be in my life. I tried to remain positive... I could do this, I told myself. I was yet to be sentenced so I conditioned my mind to accept I might be here for quite some time. Kerobokan was now my home and I had to adapt to that quickly.

Each room had a toilet, a *kaman cecil* or 'small room' with a large square-shaped bath tub filled with water that you poured over yourself with a ladle. The 'hole in the ground' toilets regularly blocked up with sewage and stank to high heaven. The block also had a barber, an Australian named Malcolm. You could get a better haircut than the one dished out to the dreadlocked guy in Block J. You could grow a beard and shave it off; grow your hair and then cut it off; give yourself a Mohawk or an undercut and experiment with your look because no one gave a fuck. I later heard that some inmates got the women and *benchong* to dye their hair different colours—they'd even do your fingernails and toenails if you wanted— because no-one cared about what anyone thought. You could choose to look clean cut or like a deranged psychopath—or both at the same time! You could also pay a modest fee to have your clothes mended. All the Indonesian prisoners tried to earn a little extra money by fixing things or doing little chores for the *bule*s.

Linga, the gang boss in charge of our block, was in Room 1 with a pair of Indonesian guys. Sandy, quite possibly the dumbest guy I met, was a member of a wealthy Indonesian family but apparently they preferred him to stay in prison rather than pay to get him out early. Room 4 was the drug room in the block, with a group of Iranians taking up Rooms 6 and 7. Two Englishmen implicated in the Lindsay Sandiford case were in Room 8, while the Russians were in Room 11. Mario, an Italian, and Hans, a German, shared a room while Chandra, the second in charge of the block, was in Room 11.

Chandra could speak English and it was easier to deal with him rather than Linga, the resident loan shark and church leader. A South African, a couple of Australians and two Japanese inmates were in the other rooms, along with Indonesians, Malays and a few Europeans.

I felt more at ease in Block B, although the conditions were just as stifling. After two months in the cell at Kuta, at least I had a room and block with other prisoners who spoke English and daily access to the outdoors and fresh air.

Like most of the inmates in Block B, the Nigerians, Michael and Lala, were convicted of drug possession. Their room was straight out of an episode of 'Pimp My Room'. They put velvet curtains with gold rings in their room, and wore sunglasses and a variety of hats. They prided themselves on being fashionable. They walked around the block all day in their Calvin Klein underwear like they were supermodels. 'Welcome to Kerobokan's Next Top Model', we'd joke. They played Jamaican music until eleven o'clock at night, but I got used to it after a while. They just didn't care about anything; they did whatever they wanted to do. They were very cool guys and warmed to me straight away. They wore suits with all the bling on to go to Mass. They were the hottest thing on Planet Kerobokan.

For the first couple of weeks I had to beg and borrow until I got access to some money. Ronald, my Indonesian mate from Kuta Police Station, would pick up money from Western Union for me that my brother wired over from the States. I kept the money in plastic bags and carried them around in the front of my shorts the entire time I was in prison. I would give Ronald 200,000 rupiah for his trouble, which was a week's wages in Bali. I made sure I took care of him because he had helped me get through the hell of Kuta Police Station and prepared me for Kerobokan.

When I was first transferred to Block B, everyone thought I must be an informant. They couldn't fathom what I was doing there.

Non-payment of hotel bills seemed a ridiculous reason to end up in Kerobokan. Some of them were sure I must be 'wired for sound' and instead of shaking my hand when we first met, an English inmate grabbed me by the shirt. 'You're "wired", mate', he hissed, but I showed him that I wasn't. I'd been framed for fraud and deception, I told them.

Despite winning their confidence in the coming weeks, some of them did not fully trust me until my situation was finally reported on the Internet the following year. That finally made the absurdity of my prison sentence as real for them as it was for me.

At night during my first week I'd sit and watch TV, drifting in and out and wondering what my next court date would bring. I knew I was going to be sentenced soon—it was just a matter of when. TV was a good distraction. There weren't any Australian shows, just Indonesian news and old action movies with Indonesian subtitles—'Rambo', Bruce Lee and old stuff like that. I think I saw 'Transformers' half a dozen times. English football was a huge hit with the block because of the westerners in there and the fact that you didn't have to speak English to understand what was going on. The World Game indeed.

CHAPTER 5

SENTENCING

I made a conscious decision very early on that no matter how long I was going to be there, I was determined to be around positive people in prison—there was a lot of negativity in Kerobokan, naturally, and I didn't want to get caught up with people who blamed others for their problems and moped around the place. I realised that I couldn't think too much about my plight and the life I led outside.

It would drive me mad. I had to stay active, stay out of trouble and not reflect too much on the ridiculous reason I was there in the first place. At least I knew that I hadn't committed a crime, I hadn't tried to smuggle drugs anywhere and I hadn't consciously hurt anyone ... just myself.

There were several other Australians in Block B: Malcolm, a tall guy from Melbourne and another guy who, like me, was originally from Western Sydney. The rest of the block appeared to look up to him. He was just hard.

The guy had a full beard and unkempt hair, and looked like a biker or Grizzly Adams. His name was Mick and he took no shit from anyone. He didn't do drugs or drink and he had no time for people who came up to him shit-faced trying to suck up to him. Many inmates asked him for money, and I often saw him give money to those who needed it and not ask for it back.

After a couple of weeks of staying with the Nigerians, Mickey suggested that I move over to his room. I continued to sleep outside, as I had done from the first night, but my name was attached to Room 3 for the rest of my stay. We became firm mates after that.

When I moved into his room with Malcolm, we were 'the Aussies'. If we had a fucking flag we would have put it on our door. If we had chalk we would have drawn a line outside our room and warned the international not to cross over in to our territorial waters.

Mickey received 18 years for attempting to smuggle 1.7 kilograms of methamphetamine into Bali in October 2010. Mick had been living in Thailand for the previous two years, where he had taught kickboxing, and told police he had borrowed the suitcase the drugs were placed into from an Indian friend named 'Peter'. The drugs were discovered when the bag was X-rayed at Denpasar airport and Mick—clean-shaven and his head completely bald—was arrested by customs.

Amphetamines are considered a Class A drug in Indonesia, and the smuggling of more than 4 kilograms of the drug known as 'ice' can result in the death penalty. The amount of drugs found in his bag was well short of that total, but they had a street value of 400,000 dollars and he was obviously in a lot of trouble. Mick enlisted the services of Schapelle Corby's solicitor and stuck to his story that he did not know the drugs were in his bag.

When Mick was pre-sentenced to 16 years in prison, he threw himself on the mercy of the court, and without admitting his guilt, apologised to the Indonesian people for bringing unwanted publicity and notoriety upon Bali. He had never been in trouble with the police before, which the AFP (Australian Federal Police) confirmed, but the court remained unmoved. Mick received 18 years—two more than his pre-sentence total.

Mick told me he had come to Bali to renew his visa. He was living in Thailand when he broke his wrist in a motorcycle accident. He was still recovering from the injury when a business associate lent him a suitcase on wheels because it was easier for him to manoeuvre. Hiding drugs inside a suitcase would have been an incredibly stupid thing to do because everyone knew the Indonesians X-rayed bags at Denpasar International airport. Mick cooperated with the police, even naming the man who lent him the bag, but the Indonesian and Thai police had no interest in investigating it.

When he was shown the drugs found in his bag, all Mick could think was, 'You bastards'. The strange thing was the drugs allegedly found were secreted behind the handle of the bag. I, along with many others, have asked how 1.7 kilograms could be secured in that small area? I don't expect people to believe that all the Australians in prison were wrongfully accused because in most cases it was stupidity that put them in prison in the first place. I know there were events in Mickey's life he regretted, as did I, but prison is a pretty lonely place to confront those issues.

In the time I knew him, Mick never wavered. If you had any bad habits like drugs or alcohol, you would certainly take them up again in prison. But Mickey never touched the stuff.

Mick had already started a Thai boxing program and a health and fitness class inside Kerobokan when I arrived there. We hit it off straight away; he was a year or two older than me, but we had grown up in the same area of Western Sydney and his brother-in- law had even attended the same high school as me.

Once I moved to Mickey's room in Block B we talked about a lot of things, especially what we were going to do with the rest of our lives when we finally got out of prison. I told him I would like to open up a clothing company. I loved designing T-shirts and surf wear. Mickey said it had long been a dream of his to open a range of retro boxing equipment—'old school' brown leather gear, not the synthetic material they use today—which he was going to call 'McQueen's'. I suppose he was a lot like the Steve McQueen character 'The Cooler King' in the classic movie 'The Great Escape' and the name just stuck. Mickey McQueen.

'Perhaps we could combine the two businesses', I suggested? 'One day', he said. One day.

Mickey knew all the inmates in Block B, as well as many of the Indonesians in the other blocks. After I got to know him a little better, Mick would tell me what each person was inside for. 'See that guy over there?' He would offer, 'He killed an Australian girl in Bali during a robbery'. I was upset when Mickey told me this. I had bought food from this guy and I got along with him okay but after hearing that I just ignored the creep. 'See that guy over there?'

Mickey would start up again. I told him I didn't want to know, and he would say, 'Just one more; you need to know this,' and he told me what many of the other prisoners did to end up in jail.

McQueen was well respected by everyone in prison, including the guards. He was a law unto himself, Mick. When the prison guards asked what religion he followed, he replied, 'Jedi'.

• • •

By this point I felt as if I'd been abandoned by both the Australian and New Zealand consulates and had been left in the hands of the Indonesian justice system. I finally made contact with the Australian consulate when they came to see the Bali Nine a week after I arrived. I sat down with an official and he asked me to tell him my story. I told him and I said I didn't care about claiming money from the government. All I wanted was an Australian passport because my existing one was going to expire while I was in Kerobokan. I needed a passport to get back to Sydney. Could he at least do that for me?

Days later, he sent me a text message saying he couldn't help me because technically, I wasn't an Australian citizen. I was a Kiwi and he washed his hands of me. He didn't even have the courtesy to call me. I tried to contact him but he wouldn't take my call.

The New Zealand consular official came to see me a couple of times. The first thing he made clear was that the New Zealand government didn't provide payments for their citizens in foreign prisons. On his first visit he bought me a packet of Oreos, on the next a packet of barbeque chips and lastly, six donuts. It was like being on 'Survivor' and winning a food challenge. I swallowed the donuts in one go. If it wasn't for my brother I'd have had no money at all.

'Where will I end up when I get out of prison?' I asked the consulate. 'In New Zealand', they said. 'But I don't live in New Zealand', I told them; 'I haven't lived there since I was a baby and I didn't know a single person there, so if you send me there, what am I going to do? My family home is in Australia'.

The consulate's reaction? 'We'll see what we can do.'

'Fuck that,' I said. 'At the end of all this, just get me on a plane back to Australia. I'll sort it out from there.'

I was in Kerobokan for almost three months before I was finally sentenced. As I made my way to court in the prison's bus, an Englishman who was being sentenced for drug possession at the same time as me leaned over and said, 'Handcuff yourself to me and you'll get your picture in the *Daily Mirror*'. I just looked at him. Are you fucking for real? As far as I knew, there was no media covering my case; there were no photos published and no one knew anything about my situation.

The bus was a large square-shaped vehicle with five steps at the back leading into a compartment area. The windows were at eye level, but whenever we stopped at traffic, the locals wouldn't make eye contact with us. They knew the bus was from Kerobokan and perhaps they were ashamed. The Western tourists however, had no problem locking their eyes on yours. Sometimes I could sense them thinking, 'You poor bastard. What did you do to get into all this trouble?'

In court, some other Westerners were drinking vodka and orange before they were sentenced. One guy was facing six years for drug smuggling and he could barely stand up he was so hammered. Some of the Indonesians on the bus with me going to court were high on crystal meth. It was not a good look and I wanted to be at my best for my judgement day.

The judge in charge of my case was, at various times

throughout the other prisoners' cases, texting, falling asleep, looking bored or laughing. But it didn't bother me because when my evidence was being put forward he kept shaking his head, as if to say, what is this man doing in here?

Finally, it was my turn to address the judge. I was either going to go off my brain and tell everyone I had been set up and the whole case against me was bullshit, which it was, or I was just going apologise to the court and accept my sentence. My interpreter pulled me aside and quietly said, 'Don't say anything to this judge; don't say too many details. Just say you're sorry'.

I decided to follow her advice. Although I knew I was completely innocent of any wrongdoing, I bit my tongue and threw myself at the mercy of the court. 'I am very sorry for what I did', I said. 'I apologise to the people of Indonesia. I brought shame on your country and I accept any punishment you are going to give me'.

The judge looked at me like I was crazy. I had thought about it a lot over the past months languishing in Kerobokan. 'I'll do my time then go home', I told myself. 'I'm 44 now, and as long as I'm out before I'm 50, I'll be happy'. I was banking on getting two and a half years. I had rolled the dice and now it was up to the judge.

The judge looked over at the prosecutor for his sentencing recommendation. 'One year!' the Indonesian prosecutor said. The judge thought long and hard and then said, '10 months'. It could have been so much worse and I was glad it was all over. 'Thank you very much,' I replied.

'The next time you come to Bali,' the judge added, 'make sure you pay your hotel bill'. And he laughed, stood up and walked off.

It was done. 'Paul', my interpreter whispered, 'I told the judge everything you told me and he believed you. He believes you are an honest person and that's why he gave you a smaller sentence'.

It wasn't until I was in Kerobokan that I was again able to talk to my brother Dave in the States. As soon as I arrived, Myu, one of the Bali Nine, gave me a phone to use.

'What happened to you?' Dave asked, wondering why I never asked him to send the final payment over.

'I took your advice', I told him. 'I told them to fuck off'.

I could hear him give a hearty laugh down the line. 'You shouldn't have told them about the 20,000-dollar loan', Dave said.

'Yeah, I stuffed up', I said. 'As soon as I said it, I knew the price of my release was going to be higher'. It was only then that he dropped a bombshell. My mother had suffered a heart attack. I was stunned. He said she was in hospital but she was alive. If my mother had died while I was sitting in a Balinese prison I would never have forgiven myself.

I talked to Dave regularly after that. There was only a certain time I could use the phone without getting caught. Usually it was about seven o'clock in the morning before the guards came in to check our block. I would text Dave that the coast was clear and he would call me back.

I didn't get to talk to my mother until her birthday, on 7 April, 2013, more than six months after I had been arrested. She was out of hospital, recovering from her heart attack. 'I never stopped worrying about you', she told me. 'I never stopped caring about you'.

I was grateful for the phone calls home. It made me feel less isolated and reminded me that on the outside there were people who were still thinking of me. I had been out of touch with my family for so long, but it was still a huge relief to hear their voices.

On the other hand, I didn't speak to Dad at all during my time in Kerobokan, not even when I got out. And as far as I know he never enquired about me. In the whole time I was there he sent me one email—he had been contacted by the consulate and they had given me Dad's phone number so I could talk to him—but it never happened. I replied to his email from prison but he never responded. I didn't know what the problem was between us and was surprised and disappointed that he seemed to care so little. Although I am an adult and we had not spoken in years I thought he might have been a little more concerned.

The reality was, when I was at my lowest point, no one could bail me out. My family dropped everything to help me, but our relationships were in such a poor state and there was nothing anyone could do to help me. I tended to get very involved in my life and before I knew it, six months had passed without talking to any members of my family. Then the six months became a year, and then two years. Phoning from America was expensive in those days, I was never a letter writer and emails were only just starting.

Dad always said we never went out for a beer or hung out like other fathers and sons, but when we did it was always very negative and I tried to avoid it as much as possible. We were never together as a family; there was always one element missing and a distance between all of us.

Maybe I'd pushed it too far with them. But then I was like that with everyone I knew, and I had always convinced myself I didn't care about the consequences. Just live your life, I told myself.

Everything will be ok!

I didn't have a wife or kids. I didn't owe anyone anything. I had no attachments and I felt as though I'd done a lot of crazy things and been on lots of adventures, so Kerobokan Prison was not going to kill me. After I was sentenced I felt mentally tough and I had always been independent.

People may think I'm crazy, but I actually grew to value my time in Kerobokan. Somewhat bizarrely, I even grew to like it. For me, Kuta was the prison. Kerobokan, on the other hand, was a chance to find out what I wanted to do with the rest of my life and what sort of person I really was.

I learned that there are really two of you in prison; the person you truly are and the person you think you are. Only one survives.

CHAPTER 6

'AFP SOLD OUT THE BALI 3X3'

While I could look forward to 'life after prison', several inmates I met in Kerobokan were living with a death sentence. The fate of the Bali Nine – Andrew Chan, Si Yi Chen, Michael Czugaj, Renae Lawrence (the only female), Tan Duc Thanh Nguyen, Matthew Norman, Scott Rush, Martin Stephens and Myuran Sukumaran – was very much in the balance when I was there.

On Sunday, 17 April 2005, Renae and Martin were arrested at Denpasar International Airport with 4.8 kilos of heroin—thought to be worth between 1 and 2 million dollars on the street—strapped to their bodies. Scott and Michael, both from Brisbane, had never met Renae and Martin before Bali, but they were there waiting for them when they were arrested and taken to the customs room. The Queensland teenagers had 3.4 kilograms of heroin taped to their bodies when they were arrested. Twenty-one-year-old Andrew Chan, thought to be one of the 'ringleaders' of the group, did not have any heroin on him when he was arrested on the plane, but he had been under close surveillance by the Indonesian National Police (INP) and Australian Federal Police (AFP).

Matthew, Tan, Si Yi and Myu were arrested at their hotel the next day. They had checked out of the Adhi Dharma Hotel the previous night and shifted to the Melasti after the others had gone to the airport to fly home. Heroin was found in their luggage after police knocked on their door and produced a search warrant. The previous day, April 17, had been Myu's 24th birthday.

The previous year, the AFP had been tipped off that a group of young Australians were planning a heroin run from Bali. The AFP already had several of the Bali Nine under surveillance, and by the time they contacted the Indonesian National Police (INP) in April 2005, they had eight names on their list... all except Myu's.

When Scott Rush's father learned his son was going to Bali—a trip he knew his son couldn't afford—he rang his barrister who then contacted the AFP. The Rushes thought their son would be warned (they were told the AFP couldn't stop Scott from going to Bali) and that it might deter Scott from taking part in any illegal activity.

None of the other parents of the Bali Nine even knew their children were in Bali.

According to published reports, it appears Tan recruited the Brisbane boys, Scott and Matthew, while Andrew was friends with Renae and Martin. Andrew worked for a catering company that serviced the Sydney Cricket Ground (SCG) and hung around the Strathfield area, where he knew Si Yi and Myu, who was a couple of years older than Andrew, from their time together at high school.

Si Yi Chen, the only son of Chinese parents, was barely 20

years old when he was arrested. One of his friends, Matthew Norman, also worked with Andrew at the SCG. The day I saw Steve Waugh score his famous last session century there in 2003, some of the future

Bali Nine drug runners were running food around the 100 or so food outlets at the SCG. Andrew, Renae, Martin and Matthew were different ages and lived in different suburbs, but they somehow came together in a joint enterprise to smuggle drugs in Bali.

There were six Western Sydney boys in Kerobokan when I was in there: Mickey McQueen, four of the Bali Nine (Andrew, Myu, Si Yi and Matty) and me. Not just six Australians, but six guys from the Western Suburbs of Sydney in a prison outside of Australia. We got on really well because we had so many similar experiences at school, at work and in pubs with our mates. They had one major difference to me, however. They all got mixed up in smuggling drugs.

Andrew Chan and Myu Sukumaran were the first Australians in history to be sentenced to the death penalty in Indonesia. All the other Bali Nine 'drug mules' originally received life sentences but four of them—Scott, Matty, Si Yi and Tan—received the death penalty on appeal in 2006. Matthew Norman was just 18 years old when he was arrested. Lawrence and Stephens received 20 years on appeal; Norman, Chen and Nguyen's sentences were commuted to life by the Supreme Court; and lastly, Scotty had his death penalty commuted to life in prison in 2011.

Those caught at the airport were known as the 'airport group' and the others as the 'Melasti group' and there was little love lost between the two after the arrests. After they were captured, the Bali Nine were held at Polda Police Station in

Denpasar—in one cell to begin with, then separately as the police tried to break them down. Surely, they would have all been pointing their fingers at each other. Andrew allegedly picked up the silver briefcase from a courier carrying almost 5 kilograms of heroin. Some were scared of Andrew and Myu, and I know Martin refused to be handcuffed to either of them when they were transported to Kerobokan.

All eight male members of the Bali Nine were initially housed in the tower block—also known as 'super maximum security'—a block of cells located at the base of a water tower, fenced, guarded and topped with barbed wire.

There are four rooms in the tower block. Andrew and Michael shared a room, Matthew had his own room, with a home gym, Myu and Si Yi shared another and Martin shared a room with Emmanuel and Tan, a Nigerian national also on death row, and a Chinese inmate. Emmanuel's case was interesting. He was caught with 400 grams of drugs in Denpasar—barely a trafficable amount compared to the Bali Nine—and he originally received 25 years in prison.

When he launched his appeal, he had no money to pay off the judges or the prosecutor and was sentenced to death.

That's justice, Indonesian style.

Scott had his own room in the tower block but he decided to move and share a cell with six other Indonesian prisoners in Block K when I was there. I have no idea why he moved out of the tower, but then Scotty is a law to himself. He likes to think that he can blend in with the other prisoners—'Scotty Rush, the white chameleon, in no rush to be seen', I remarked to him one day and he laughed—but he can't escape his past or what he did to end up in Kerobokan. It continually plays on his mind and eats away at his hopes for the future.

The tower block also contained a 'cell tikus' or 'rat cell', one of a number of dark solitary confinement cells in Kerobokan. These cells were used to house inmates who wouldn't or couldn't comply with prison rules. The guards threw prisoners in there and forced them to pay them off to be let out. Conditions in 'cell tikus' were far worse than any other cell in the prison. There was no toilet, so inmates would have to crap in a plastic bag and throw it out the front, and there was nothing else in there except a six-foot concrete bunk. To me that was a real prison. Inhumane is too nice a word for that cell. It was worse than hell! There were prison guards there to protect the Bali Nine in 'maximum security', but the gangs could easily walk around the corner past the main canteen and yell to them through the fence.

Andrew Chan was a very positive guy. He was very loyal—a leader who commands respect—and nothing like the street gangster portrayed in the media. He had all these stories about when he was younger and when he was in the gangs. I didn't want to hear about them, but he'd say, 'Paul, I just want to tell you one thing . . .' So I'd listen to him because he was such a good talker. He was never negative—he didn't even swear—and he tried to get along with everyone.

Andrew was thoughtful and quick to offer his take on other prisoners. He had a larrikin smile, and loved to talk. He supported the Penrith Panthers rugby league team and had a few noticeable scars that show he got into the odd scrap during his time on the streets of Western Sydney. He could be spontaneous and analytical when he put his mind to it. Inside prison, he found something purposeful out of a nightmarish situation. He spoke fluent Indonesian, and where the other members of Bali Nine battled anxiety and depression, Andrew harnessed whatever fear he has and appeared confident to the point of cockiness. When I last saw him, he was trying to remain positive in a situation that had very little upside.

Andrew never talked about regrets. I know he apologised to the others for getting them mixed up in it. That didn't help too much, because they're all still in there, but at least he did it. I never talked to him about what happened in Bali and I think he appreciated that. I took him at face value, not for what he did. I did that with all of the Bali Nine boys, and I think that's one of the reasons we all got on so well.

When Andrew first came into Kerobokan he was 'lost' as a person. But he did many good things for others, he got people to care about him and he started to appreciate life.

Scotty was from a good family, lived in a good home and went to a good school, but went off the rails as a teenager and drifted into drugs. He too struggled in prison when he first arrived because he had no one to talk to. Scotty was always popular with visitors and he even had a cyber 'stalker' for a while. Unfortunately, one of Scott's friends had pulled a pretty hilarious, if cruel, prank on him. They created a fake Facebook profile of a hot young girl who contacted Scotty saying she was interested in coming to visit. When Scotty saw the picture of a hot chick he was all excited and looking forward to her arrival. It was actually one of the other guys in the tower.

They kept it going long enough but eventually they had to tell him the news it was a fake.

Scotty was devastated and Michael, his Bali Nine co-accused, told everyone it was a cruel thing to do.

I spent a lot of time in Andrew's room, watching the

interactions between the members of the Bali Nine. Andrew kept two pet cobras. I asked him why he kept such unusual pets and he said it was because the Indonesian guards were scared of snakes and they would leave him alone. Scotty had a pet turtle named Crush. When he was sitting on the floor watching TV, Andrew would sit on his bed behind Scotty, grab the turtle and rub its belly with a toothbrush. This aggravated the turtle and it would start nipping and biting. Andrew would then put the turtle next to Scotty's arm and the turtle would bite him through his T-shirt. There seemed to be a good camaraderie there for a while, but that doesn't appear to be the case now.

In his outside life, Myu would have started his own business—a café, a restaurant, a video shop. Myu was doing his best to be productive in prison and, like Andrew, to help others. Not nearly as confident or outgoing as Andrew, Myu has also struggled to come to terms with where he is. It was very hard to strike up a conversation with him at times, but he was keen to train with me and he became a frequent visitor to the Block B gym. Myu often had a thousand- mile stare on his face; as if he was somewhere else or thinking of something else far, far away.

Myu organised all the art and craft made inside the prison and paid for all the materials from the sale of the items. The girls in the women's prison decided that they wanted to paint in their block, but when they tried to sell their paintings outside Myu wouldn't allow it. The girl who organised this was named Gina, the girlfriend of Mario who was with me in Block B. Myu had warned Gina to stop, but when a shipment of paints and canvases arrived they never reached the women's block because Myu told the guards to stop them at the front door.

The following story shows how quickly things can get out of hand in prison. When Gina complained to her boyfriend Mario about Myu stopping her art materials from coming into the prison, Mario called Myu a 'black monkey' and threatened to get even.

This quickly got back to Myu, who stormed into our block, itching for a fight. Mario backed down, but when the Nigerians heard the argument, they originally backed Mario and told Myu not to come into Block B making problems. When Myu told them why he was angry, the Nigerians turned on Mario.

'Are we black monkeys too?' they demanded. And the fight was on! The whole situation changed 180 degrees in a split second.

Myu ran the painting studio, he had a jewellery shop and he had a printing shop for making T-shirts. He also made surfboards there for a while. Inmates who worked for Myu were paid in food so they always had lunch and dinner available, but they couldn't make any money. Myu also had computers in his block, in a room they called 'The Bengkar'. The computers didn't have Internet access and could only be used for graphic design and word processing. This being Kerobokan, however, when it poured with rain the computer room would flood and ruin all the computers.

A Malaysian guy named Boo became the drug boss in Room 4 in our block. Boo also worked in the jewellery shop with Si Yi. They had a scale that weighed all the silver in the shop, so Boo decided to take it back to Room 4 and weigh the drugs with it. The police came in one morning and raided Room 4 and took the scales. Si Yi didn't even know Boo had them. The next day Boo confessed to Si Yi and he barred him from the jewellery shop. Boo came to me and asked if I could please talk to them because he liked working there and making silver jewellery.

'Mate, what can I do?' I said. 'You're barred, that's it'.

The Australian Government gives its citizens in Kerobokan 120 dollars a month (1.2 million rupiah) each. They have to live on that much money, with the idea being they have to pay it back when they get out. The money goes a long way. Most of the Bali Nine have nice beds with spring mattresses, plasma TVs and Nintendo games— all paid for by the Australian government, bought by their family or donated by supporters. But to say, as some reports do, that they 'live like kings', is wrong. Try living in a third-world prison with the death penalty or a life sentence hanging over your head and see if you feel like a king.

Renae and Martin were very close, even though they were in separate sections of the prison. They had the same legal team for a while and were held together at Polda Police Station after they were arrested. Marty really looked out for Renae in prison. A warm, big-hearted guy, Marty was almost 30 when he was captured, considerably older than then others, and had told his family he was going to Darwin to deliver furniture for a mate. His parents turned on the television and saw him in handcuffs in Bali. He is engaged to an Indonesian woman now who already had a couple of kids and he hopes to be released early.

It would seem natural that two of the highest-profile Australian female prisoners would have become friends, but it appeared that Renae was not particularly close to Schapelle Corby. Renae originally formed an alliance with Schapelle after being caught harming herself by slashing her wrists with the ring pull of a soft drink can. She was in a fragile state of mind for a while, but she was able to gather a few Indonesian female prisoners under her wing and seemed to have found a purpose in prison.

Renae was in a relationship with a woman with three young children, but it ended a year before she went to Bali, in April 2005. The collapse of the relationship seemed to have tipped her over the edge. Renae's naturally quiet, with a high-pitched voice that goes against her tough-looking exterior. At first she wouldn't even say hello to me. That's just the way it is, I told myself; some inmates don't want to talk to people who are in there for a short time. It wasn't until a few months later, when I sat next to her and Schapelle at the Christmas party, that I got to know them both a little better.

One of the funniest things I saw in Kerobokan happened one day when I was sitting outside with some of the guys from Block B and spotted Renae walking out of the women's block with an angle grinder. We could hear the angle grinder in her room, so she was obviously building something in there. A few minutes later she came back and grabbed a huge pick and walked past us again. We could hear her smashing concrete in the women's block. We all started laughing. It was bizarre. I had to ask the obvious question. 'Do you think Renae is escaping?'

I was shocked to hear Renae was shifted out of Kerobokan in October 2013 after being implicated in an alleged plot to murder a prison guard. This 'plot' apparently came to light when a search of the women's cell block allegedly found Blackberry messages between Renae and a notorious inmate known as 'Black Sonia' or 'Black Monster' discussing killing a guard. All this happened while Renae was in hospital having her appendix removed.

Renae and Black Monster were quickly transferred to Negara Jail in Jembrana in West Bali. Renae had become the senior female prisoner in Kerobokan—even over Schapelle Corby—but this new charge meant she would be stripped of any remissions she may have earned in the past year. Black Monster is a notorious East Timorese inmate of Kerobokan. Famously, she gave birth to a baby in prison after a late night tryst with a Scottish prisoner, which was organised by a prison guard who 'wanted to watch'. The sex act was consummated through the bars of the women's compound. The baby was born with fair skin, blue eyes and blond hair and was cared for by the parents of the Scottish father, until Sonia was again jailed and she allegedly sold the baby to the family of another inmate for four bags of *shabu* (crystal meth).

Black Monster had been in and out of Kerobokan on charges of seducing, drugging and then robbing male tourists, and found her way back into prison on the charge of kidnapping the baby of a French family in Bali. She was psychotic, unhinged and dangerous. Placed in cell tikus, she famously faked her own hanging, and when the guard came in the following morning, almost scared him half to death before attacking him.

There's no way Renae would have had anything to do with Black Monster. The whole story is bullshit, made up by the prison system to take away any power Renae may have acquired in more than eight years in prison.

The Bali Nine might be a tourist novelty but back in Australia they don't receive the public sympathy that Schapelle Corby does. Schapelle doesn't look like a drug smuggler and she has always denied the marijuana found on her was hers. In contrast, the Bali Nine were caught red handed with the drugs wrapped around their bodies and openly admitted their guilt. 'Will we get the death sentence?' one of them asked within the first hour they were arrested. The drugs they were importing would have ruined many lives. But I suspect that anyone who got to know them as people— especially Andrew and Myu who were on death row—could not have been moved by their situation or be impressed by the potential they could have had on the outside. Not nearly as confident or outgoing as Andrew, Myu has also struggled to come to terms with where he is.

Many people have wondered why the AFP would tip off a foreign country to a possible crime that carries the death penalty, and not intervene earlier to stop the crime from being carried out. Obviously they didn't have all the names of the 'players' in the heroin run and wanted to also capture the source of the drugs, which was thought to have been brought into Bali by a young Indonesian woman. The AFP followed their guidelines, they said. But even allowing for the 'information swapping' that happens between law agencies, many can't believe they didn't ask the Indonesian government to withdraw the death penalty for the Bali Nine in exchange for providing the information that led to their arrests.

The AFP remains unapologetic about their actions and has said that if the same circumstances happened tomorrow they would do exactly the same thing. They are fighting a war on drugs, they say, and fair enough. They are putting more and more resources into stopping the drug trade at the source before it gets into Australia. Drug smuggling constitutes a vicious, vicious trade in human suffering. And because the situation was being played out on Indonesian soil, I imagine the Indonesians were in charge of the show with the AFP on the sidelines, watching and waiting. Who knows? But I think they should have done more.

I believe if the Indonesian government executed any of the Bali Nine there would be a massive uproar in Australia. They're hostages really, not prisoners, and, in my opinion, they're the only thing Indonesia has to hold over Australia. If Indonesia executes any of the Bali Nine inmates they would be left with no cards to play in political negotiations with their most powerful neighbour.

When I was partying in Bali before my arrest in August 2012, I saw the following graffiti on the wall of an abandoned shop: 'AFP sold Out Bali 3x3'. Harsh? Many, including some of the parents of the Bali Nine, don't think so.

CHAPTER 7

TUNA-FREE DOLPHIN AT THE KEROBOKAN CANTEEN

Where were no rules when you were on holiday in Bali. You could do what you liked and no one gave a fuck. It was a dangerous way to think, but it was an insight into the absolute fascination Westerners have for the Indonesian island... that complete sense of freedom and recklessness; the powerful feeling of being kings in a third-world country.

It's amazing how a five-hour flight to Bali can change your whole perspective on life. Your personality changes once you are there, you let your hair down and you get away with shit you just can't do at home. Ride a motorbike without a helmet? No problem. Responsible service of alcohol? What's that? Are the women easy? Yes, you just have to ask... or pay.

The strange thing was that you could go and sit in a bar in Bali and the guy next to you would be just as excited as you to be there. A guy who wouldn't give you the time of day in a pub at home would become your best mate for the night in Bali. Why is that?

Me? I'd talk to anyone. I found the Aussie girls somewhat up themselves in Bali. They were easy pickings for the local guys and foreigners because they weren't interested in Aussie guys. Fair enough, perhaps. The European girls were great fun and so hot, especially the Swedish girls, but the local women also got a look in. They were very exotic, and when they rode past on their motorbikes, damn they looked sexy, but you had to be careful. The 'Indo' girls told you what you wanted to hear, but you soon realised that most of it was bullshit.

A lot of the locals are desperate to make money out of the Westerners and will think nothing of tricking you or scamming you out of your money. But people on holiday there tend only to see the 'paradise'... not the filth and the poverty and the crime.

I must have gone to Bali more than 30 times in the three years I worked at Qantas. The place became very familiar too me, but naïvely I never wondered too much about the other side of the party island... the dark side. I knew that you didn't touch the local marijuana or shabu, *but I knew nothing of the drug trade that operated out of the island and the criminals who lived there off the proceeds of trafficking drugs.*

That was to come much later.

I kept in contact with Dad while I was living in the States in the 1990s—he even came and visited us once after Dave came over and settled down. I rented a house for a while with my car dealership colleague Bruce. He had befriended a lot of Canadians who travelled the country paving US freeways—many of them were ex-hockey players—and whenever there was a hockey game in town we would party with famous NHL players. I met a lot of sportspeople while selling cars at Newport Beach, especially gridiron footballers who were cashed up and ready to splash out on a Wrangler.

I was in a stable relationship in the States for seven years, but when that broke down in the late 1990s I decided to return to Australia. Mum had moved east because she was sick of the West Coast. I was sick of the States by then too; the whole place was fake. The Americans were always talking themselves up, it seemed, boasting about what they owned and what they earned, but they never shouted a drink out of turn. It was always 'buy me a beer and I will tell you a story'. No thanks. I'll buy my own beer and you can keep your story to yourself.

When I left America in 1998, I found I had a problem with my passport as soon as I went to the Qantas counter. I was a Kiwi national with a British passport because my Dad is British. I had always wanted to play soccer in England so I always kept my dual citizenship, despite the fact that I considered myself, for all intents and purposes, an Australian. My British passport had expired while I was in America and I had it renewed before I decided to go home, but home for me was Sydney. I bought a plane ticket for Sydney but when I got to LA International Airport they took one look at my passport and said, 'Sorry sir, but you can't fly to Sydney because you don't have a resident's visa'.

I'd neglected to get the right visa. There must be some way around this, I told them.

I missed my flight to Sydney and there were no other flights that night. I studied the flight board at the airport the following morning for somewhere I could go on my existing visa. There was a flight to Bali, of all places, and they said I could sort out my visa problems to get back into Australia once I was there. I went straight to the Garuda desk and bought a ticket for 2,500 dollars, which was a hell of a lot of money at that time, but I was desperate. I was in Bali for two months, and in that time I went to the New Zealand consulate to sort it all out. They suggested I talk to the Aussies if I wanted to fly to Sydney.

The Australian consulate said I had to go to their Sydney office to obtain an entry visa. After I landed in Sydney, I went straight to the immigration office and they said because I wasn't a permanent

Australian resident any more they couldn't give me residency. 'Listen', I told them, 'I just renewed my passport; I only forgot to get my visa. I am a fucking Australian', I said. 'I was born in New Zealand but I have lived in Sydney from the age of six months. I worked for Qantas and paid my taxes, I insisted, and got mad and said I wanted that fucking visa stamped now.

And it worked. The manager came out and apologised and granted me a visa on the spot. That's all I ever wanted, I told them, and I walked out of the office.

• • •

We were only fed twice a day in Kerobokan, once in the morning and again at night. I'm a big guy, 6 foot tall and over 110 kilograms, and I was always hungry because the food was such poor quality that my general health and nutrition went downhill fast. I even started to pull my toenails out. Sitting there with nothing to do, and without any clippers, I would pick them until they came out.

I don't know if it was the diet, or the poor quality water, but my toenails just chipped off and came out altogether. We didn't wear shoes around Kerobokan, just sandals, so our feet were really damaged.

Many prisoners bought food from the canteen at the front of the prison, or from outside the prison, and cooked it on gas stoves and camp ovens in their cells. We often pooled our money and bought and cooked our own food. We were lucky to have Lief, a professional chef from Sweden, in our block, and against our better judgment when he was high as a kite, we would put him in charge of cooking a special meal for everyone. The first time we did this, he burned the rice.

How could a professional chef burn rice?

Mario tried to grow herbs in foam boxes outside our makeshift kitchen, with some success. Some of the Iranians in our block grew tomatoes and lettuces in a garden behind our block. The gangs even grew some weed out there. We bent two of the steel bars of the block so they pointed to the sky, Superman-style, and some of us were able to squeeze through and tend to the garden. The guards turned a blind eye to this because when our toilets blocked up we had to go into this field and clean up the sewage which had spilled all over the soil. This helped the garden, but after one of the Indonesians escaped from the prison through a break in one of the walls, the guards told us we had to ask permission to go 'out the back' from then on.

One of the Russians in our block had a girlfriend who lived just down the road from the prison so once or week we'd ask her to bring in Burger King as a treat. On every other Saturday we'd buy pizza—and I know this sounds cliché because I laughed at it myself when I was told—because Al the Mafia boss, a fellow inmate, had a best friend who owned an Italian restaurant in Kuta. One week we'd splurge out on a large pizza and then the next week we'd have Burger King. That was our weekly treat; we'd save up our money and pig out for one day a week. It felt great. We'd have nothing until the next visit but we just wanted to feel the sensation of having stuffed ourselves with food.

The guards would also get food for you from the outside... for a fee. They would even deliver it to your cell. All you had to do was order the takeaway food on your phone—the phone you weren't allowed to have in prison—and the shop would deliver it to the front gate. The guards would drag it through the bars and bring it to your cell. You had to go into your cell, shut your door and eat it in peace because the sight and smell of food from outside the prison would always attract a crowd. In the middle of the night you'd hear someone opening a packet of chips and all these heads would pop up like meerkats. What was that? Food? Everyone was so hungry the slightest rustle of paper would set everyone off.

We talked about different food from around the world, sharing our stories of the best meals we ever had, and I'm sure it was a form of therapy for some of us. One of the *bule*s had access to so much money he kept a personal chef in work outside every day to cook food for him and drop it off at the front gate.

That's luxury, Kerobokan style.

Not that all the food ordered from the outside made it to our cells. The guards were known for eating prisoners' food. I desperately wanted some tuna and I asked my friend Virginia, an Australian lady who ran an orphanage in Bali, if she could bring in a can for me. The guards stopped her at the front gate. 'No, no, no,' they told her, 'You can't bring that in'. When she asked why, the guards confiscated it. The next day, Virginia came back to the jail and asked the guard if she could take the tuna into me and she was again told no. When she asked where the tuna was, the guard pointed to his mouth.

'You ate my tuna?' she asked. It was unbelievable. Only in Kerobokan!

The guards would either confiscate food at the front gate or they would let you through, but by the time you had collected your food and tried to walk out to go back into your block there would be eight guards there and they would hit you up for what you had. They'd grab an apple or an orange or a packet of biscuits out of your stash as 'payment'. They were absolute scavengers.

None of the *bules* ate the breakfast handed out daily. On some days the bread was really fresh, and on other days it was hard as cardboard. Often the bananas were a black, mushy mess. I had to check the rice because I would often find little rocks in it that would chip my teeth. The Indonesians said this was because they put the rice on the ground to dry it and then rolled it up in a ball to cook it. Tiny rocks, small sticks and even broken glass then got caught up with it. I couldn't comprehend that. Why not clean the ground before you put the rice on it? They didn't care. The food they supplied us would go off in a couple of hours. The eggs were brown and inedible. Just thinking about them now makes me sick.

Luckily, Kerobokan also had a canteen. At the canteen, we could purchase the edible food the prison should have been feeding us at breakfast and dinner. I used to go the canteen in the morning to buy a piece of pineapple for 10c and it was good. I'd eat five pieces of fruit for breakfast and had a big cup of tea and I was set for the day.

The canteen was run by an Indonesian called Farouk, who was also our block's 'accountant' and collected our money to pay the big boss for our food and rent. You could buy almost anything from Farouk: bottled water, cold drinks, coffee and tea, ice cream and food... good food, edible food, hot food! The only problem was that it was the worst-run canteen in the world. If it operated as a business on the outside, not only would it go broke, despite the fact that Farouk marked his prices up by 1000 per cent, but the health and hygiene officers would close it down in a heartbeat (if there was such a thing in Bali). A large Indonesian lady who worked in the canteen would often spit on the floor as she cooked. Real classy...

When I arrived in the oppressive heat of Kerobokan, I thought a bottle of fresh, cold water would be a godsend. I assumed it was commercially bottled water but it wasn't.

The canteen staff filled up old bottles using a tap near the fish pond. The meant that much of the bottled water came from the bore under the prison. If I left a bottle of water out in the sunlight for a couple of days it would turn white because of all the calcium in the bore water, which ate away at my clothes over time and caused my teeth to become really sensitive. There was no way I was going to drink it when I could see all the calcium flakes floating in the water. And that's not the only thing I found floating. There was cigarette ash in one of the bottles I bought from the canteen. They didn't even have the decency to rinse the bottle out before they refilled it with tap water and sold it for 2,000 rupiah, which is about 20 cents. At least cigarette ash wouldn't kill me. After the Kerobokan inmate riots of February 2012, asbestos from the prison walls got into the water system and Bali Nine Matthew told me that everyone broke out in a rash.

After I heard that I never bought water from the canteen again.

The canteen would often run out of items—popular things like soft drinks and cigarettes—waiting until they had totally run out before ordering more. 'It's a prison, you idiots', I would rail at them when they ran out, frustrated by their lack of foresight. 'Everyone wants cigarettes or a cold drink. All you have to do is order more and you'll sell more. It's a very simple system'. They, of course, didn't understand this. All they would say was 'We sold out!'

I would often order food from the canteen and nothing would come, despite the fact that I would be the only one there at the time. Sometimes I would order at two o'clock in the afternoon and they would bring it four hours later, at about six o'clock, so I never knew how long it had been sitting there in the heat.

One night when I did get the meal I ordered, I was sitting there chewing what I thought was a chicken bone and when I pulled it out and put it on the plate, it made a metallic sound. I picked it up and stared at it. It was a nail! Imagine if that went through my digestive system. It would have ripped my insides out. It happened twice while I was in Kerobokan and I thought for sure someone was deliberately trying to sabotage our meals. The canteen also served food with staples in it. The staples would be used to secure the brown paper bag the food was delivered in. The word was that one of the Indonesian gang members threw a handful of staples in the food to try to sabotage the canteen.

By the end of my time in prison, I was taking every opportunity to take the piss out of the Indonesians who ran the canteen. 'What you want?' they'd ask.

'How about some tuna-free dolphin?' I'd say.

'What?' They wouldn't know what I was talking about. 'You've heard of dolphin-free tuna?' I said.

'What?' they'd say. Oh, forget about it.

Anywhere else, the Kerobokan canteen would go out of business in a day. But this was prison and they had a captive audience.

Despite being useless at running a business, Farouk presented as a genuinely nice guy. We later learned he was in prison because he stabbed his girlfriend to death. While in prison he had also, over time, stolen about a million rupiah from the canteen. McQueen and I confronted him about it one day, demanding our money back from him. Farouk sat with his knees crossed, rocking back and forth nervously. 'We want to know where the fucking money is?' we demanded. 'Now!' Farouk's eyes rolled back into his head. He had drifted into a trance. 'This is probably the psychotic state he was in when he murdered his girl', McQueen said. You could tell he was just going to explode.

The best canteen was in Block F, the block run by Indonesian gangs. They obviously had better quality-control procedures. Stuff up the canteen and they bashed the shit out of you. Perhaps no one was brave enough to complain. The guy who ran the canteen was pretty 'famous' among all the Indonesians in prison. He reportedly broke into a home, killed the husband, raped his wife and then killed her and her infant son. Real 'businessman of the year' material there. I could understand why no one complained.

Lief and Mario—who being Italian also fancied his culinary skills—decided to make their own food in direct competition to the canteen. The Indonesian gangs in the other blocks weren't happy about it because it was breaking the monopoly they had on selling food. 'We're not going to eat this shit anymore,' we said. 'Our shit is better!'

It wasn't.

Lief and Mario bought in meat from the outside and started selling food at the back of the kitchen, but they had no more of an idea of how to run a canteen than the Indonesians. All they did was cook food to sell so they could buy drugs. But the cost of their drug habit soon outstripped their income so they raised the prices. No one bought their food and the boys couldn't work out why. I kept telling them they were charging too much money.

'Yeah', Mario reasoned, 'but the canteen's food is shit'. 'But mate', I tried to explain to him, 'your food is five bucks and the canteen sells it for eighty cents. Your food isn't *that* good!'

Lief and Mario then decided to go into the hamburger business. They ordered all the ingredients from the outside and announced we were all going to have hamburgers to eat every Sunday. We thought this was a great idea and asked how much they were. '50,000 rupiah each', they said. 'I can get two whoppers from Burger King from outside the prison for that much money', I told them. They kept on reasoning that the hamburgers they were making would cost 75,000 rupiah on the 'outside'. 'What's wrong with you?' I said. 'We're not outside. We're in prison! Who gives a fuck what they charge outside? People don't have 50,000 rupiah in prison for a hamburger when you can go and buy a canteen meal for 8,000'.

They wouldn't listen. They went ahead and cooked sixty hamburgers and they sold barely a dozen. They had loads of hamburgers left over and they wasted a lot of food and money. They ended up handing them out free to everybody but I didn't want any. I was too annoyed with them to eat their food.

Their business was not helped by the fact that their products would often be stolen before they could be sold. We had wooden cabinets at the back of the common room in which we put all our personal things. We would have a key so we could lock them and we referred to them as our 'villas'... our property. That's prison humour when you have absolutely nothing to your name. Mario bought little packets of coffee in strips of ten that he planned to sell individually. We had them locked up in his cupboard and someone came in at night and took them. I think it was the block next door.

Nothing was sacred in Kerobokan.

CHAPTER 8

THE USUAL SUSPECTS

As my time inside the prison passed from weeks to months, I learnt that every prisoner had a story and a past, but would they have a future? Most of the *bule*s I was with in Block B were in their late thirties or early forties—guys around the same age as me. But, unlike me, their lives had been shattered by drugs. They had decades to serve in prison and their hopes and dreams would always be left unfulfilled. Some of the guys I met during my time at Kerobokan became close friends, some of them I avoided when I could and some of them were completely insane.

Alberto was a lovely guy, and so polite. Every morning, he would say 'good morning Paul' and I'd reply in kind. I'd buy him a coke, and he'd buy me one back. If he couldn't eat all of his pizza, he'd offer me a piece. A salt of the earth guy, Al. He was Italian and he was the closest thing to the *real* Mafia in Kerobokan.

The Indonesian gangs respected Alberto because, although they thought they were mafia, they really weren't, and Al was the real deal from Sicily. I later heard he was in prison for ten years in Italy and when he got out he fled the country because the wrong people were after him. Al was hiding in Bali and was trying to organise a passport to fly out of the country. Apparently, his friend was only days away from coming over to see him when he was caught. He said that it was the Russians who reported him to Interpol. They knew who he was and where he was and the Russians let him know it. 'Send us five grand and we won't tell the authorities', the Russians told him. Apparently, they kept the money and reported him anyway.

Alberto was the most innocuous looking guy; he looked like someone out of 'The Big Bang Theory', a real 'Poindexter' with thick glasses and a beaky nose. Nothing like a mafia tough guy... more like Pee Wee Herman than Michael Corleone from the movie 'The Godfather'. Alberto didn't have to be a tough guy because he could make a call any time he liked and hire a tough guy to do the dirty work for him. He didn't physically demand respect, like Mickey or some of the bigger guys, it was just given to him on reputation.

Malcolm was a 'six-footer' from Melbourne who famously did the bolt from a Bali police car when he was arrested at the airport on suspicion of carrying drugs internally. When he was recaptured, they put him in a hospital room with a doctor to X-ray him. Malcolm said he should have bribed the doctor to switch the X-rays and he would have walked free. 'Why didn't you punch the shit out of the doctor and escape through a window?' McQueen asked. 'There were no police in there with you'.

'Yeah', was all Malcolm could meekly offer in reply.

It was impossible to carry on a conversation with Malcolm

because he was always off his face on Xanax. He was looking forward to going home soon, but he told me it wouldn't be on a Qantas jet. He was banned from flying on Qantas because he was 'coked' off his head on a flight from India and ended up knocking someone out.

Malcolm, McQueen and I were sharing the same room when Alberto arrived in Kerobokan, but the gangs who run the prison kicked Malcolm out and put Alberto in with us. We think they wanted McQueen to take care of him and protect him because they respected McQueen and they respected Al before he even came into the prison. I was already sleeping out on the floor and Malcolm joined me in the common area for three weeks until they found him a new room.

The only person Alberto truly liked and respected in Kerobokan was McQueen, probably because McQueen knew a little Italian and could talk to him in his own language. Maybe it was also because McQueen just tells it how it is and Alberto was the same way.

Neither of them put up with any bullshit.

I used to train with McQueen quite a lot and we would spend hours boxing together in the gym. When I say 'gym', I'm not talking about a state of the art gymnasium you find in a shopping centre or industrial area in the suburbs. This was the worst gym in the world in the worst place in the world. The barbells were made out of metal off-cuts and concrete weights set in plastic flower pots. The boxing gloves had been donated, but they were thin and worn. Instead of padded benches, we lay down on a wooden bench covered in cow- hide.

While we were training one day, McQueen called out to Alberto, 'Al, you've got to do some training, mate... do some weights and some exercises'. Al's reply to McQueen was comically menacing. 'I only do one exercise', he said. He then pointed his finger like a gun and moved his index finger like a trigger.

Alberto told us the story of when he was being held in Polda Police Station. Al's cell was raided by the prison guards. They confiscated all his possessions, including a laptop computer he used to conduct all his 'business' on the outside. The guards were going through his computer files but, fortunately for Al, the guard who was looking into it saw the bed in the cell and decided to have an afternoon siesta. Al then snuck into his own room, deleted all the incriminating evidence on his computer and poured a glass of water over the keyboard to ruin the computer. The guards were so inept they didn't think to take the computer to a different room, or even to try and stay awake while searching for evidence.

There were two Peters in our block: 'Old Peter' and 'German Peter'. Old Peter was an elderly guy with a pacemaker, a Mohawk haircut and tattoos all over him who looked like the John Hurt character in the movie Midnight Express. He became a good friend of mine and I'm still in contact with him. He's an ex member of a biker gang who has travelled the world, loves his crack pipe and took every conceivable narcotic in jail—marijuana, *shabu*, heroin—you name it, he did it.

The story I heard was he had eight marijuana seeds in his pocket when customs officials searched him 'on spec' at the airport. They gave him five years and threw him in Kerobokan. Peter said he had terminal cancer, so he wrote a letter to the Indonesian President and asked for clemency and they reduced his sentence to three and a half years. He was always sick in prison, but he served his time and when he went to the front office on his release day, they said he had to pay an 80,000-dollar fine or he had to stay inside for another three months.

80,000 dollars! His reply? 'I'll stay another three months'.

The other Peter was a skinny little German guy who smoked pot all day. He lived in Java with his Indonesian wife and their young daughter but he decided to come to Bali for a holiday by himself and he bought some weed. He was smoking dope in his room when the fumes were smelled outside and the cops were called. The police came in and busted him and threw him in Kerobokan for a year.

When I came across him in prison I found him curled up in a foetal position on the ground, crying like a baby.

Peter just couldn't handle life in prison. He continually broke down. I'd be at the canteen and he'd be crying; 'Paul, I don't know if I can make it'. I reminded him that he was only in prison for a year and there were other people in there doing life sentences, so stop crying for fuck's sake. It wasn't the end of the world.

I thought this was pretty sound advice. But it got worse for Peter. His family came to visit him at Christmas and his wife told him she didn't want him back, she was taking all his money and selling his house and he wouldn't see his daughter anymore.

That certainly shook him up and the crying spells intensified. 'Tell her to fuck off', I told him, tired of hearing him complain. It was better than some of the other advice he got from inside the block—advice involving guns and knives and hunting her down and burning the house to the ground. I actually felt a bit a bit of sympathy for the poor guy for a while. But I later found out the reason Peter moved to Java in the first place was because he was busted with 30 kilograms of marijuana in Germany and had to leave the country.

Peter wasn't made for prison and everything he did only made it worse for himself. He slept on the bottom bunk and every time he stood up he hit his head on the top bunk. In the middle of the night, he would get up to go to the toilet and hit his head every time. A prisoner we called Gopes decided to bang some nails to hang down from the top bunk of the bed. We told him he couldn't do that because the nail would go into Peter's skull.

'Well, it's the only way I'm going to teach him', was Gopes' reply. Peter's weed addiction got him into a lot of trouble in Kerobokan.

Once he asked Michael, one of the Nigerians, to sell him some weed. 'I've only got 500,000 rupiah worth of weed', Michael replied. Peter said he didn't want that much weed, but Michael told him 'Well, that's all I've got. Take it or leave it'. And so he took it. Peter gave him 500,000 rupiah before seeing any weed and Michael went and paid off a debt he owed to Emmanuel.

Peter came back later to collect his weed and Michael said he didn't have any in the first place and that he had used the money to pay off his debt to Emmanuel. Unbelievably, Peter then walked up to Emmanuel demanding his money back. Emmanuel laughed and just replied, 'Michael owed me 500,000 rupiah so I don't give a fuck about you or your weed. It's prison!' Peter was strung out for a week because he didn't have any weed to smoke and he had lost his money, so he threw a brick at Michael and ended up in cell tikus.

German Peter was his own worst enemy. He bought a

bottle of Scotch for his birthday and he left it in the kitchen where Lief and Mario found it. 'If this bottle's still here in ten minutes, we're going to crack the top off it', Lief said. 'And once we crack the top we're going to drink the lot'. And that's exactly what they did. I went to boxing training and came back an hour later and Lief and Mario were blind drunk on the ground.

When Peter came back he asked everyone, 'Where's my Scotch?' He couldn't make the connection that Lief and Mario were drunk right in front of him and his Scotch was missing, but when he found out he was furious. 'You're stupid for leaving it lying around,' I told him. 'Why didn't you go and hide it somewhere?'

He went away for about half an hour to sulk and then came back carrying a birthday cake. Peter had bought himself a birthday cake, cut it up into slices and was handing it out to everyone who had just been laughing at him and drinking his Scotch. McQueen and I just looked at him, shocked. 'Have some self respect and harden up!' we told him. He couldn't stand up for himself. He just got trampled on and everyone ripped him off.

The Iranians in our block were given life sentences for smuggling drugs. There were three of them in one room and four in another.

They had no access to money and they hardly ate. One of them was named Ali and he used to wander around the prison like a zombie. If I asked him how he was, he would just point to his head and say, 'sick, sick'. One day, Ali came out of his stupor and walked up to me with wide eyes, and right into my face, yelled, 'You fucking talking about me, I can hear you!' McQueen and I were just sitting there, minding our own business. 'What are you talking about, mate?' we asked. He just mumbled incoherently and wandered off. Ali was harmless, but you never turned your back on him.

There were a lot of prisoners like Ali taking crystal meth and the scary thing was that you never knew what people in prison were capable of when under the influence of drugs. It certainly put me on my guard every day.

One of the most eccentric characters in the block was a Russian called Sanchez. Sanchez had a habit of blessing everything, including his bed after he made it each morning and his cigarettes before he lit up. We called him Mick Jagger because he looked like the Rolling Stones frontman when he strutted around the block in his tight pants without his shirt on.

Serge, also Russian, had no idea what was happening to him. He still thought he was waiting to go to court, but he had already received his sentence and he was serving eleven years. 'It's done and dusted', I tried to explain to him. 'You got 11 years. It's on the Internet'. He couldn't comprehend and still thought he was going to be released soon. Poor bastard.

Another Russian, Rizzo, slept all day and stayed up all night. 'I can't go out during the day, it's too light', he said. 'I only like the night'.

'Are you a vampire?' I asked. 'Do you hang from the ceiling when you sleep?' He didn't get the joke. Rizzo was supposed to get six months, but his lawyer fucked him over and he got five years. The Russians smoked so much dope they may as well have been on another planet, but they were good poker players. Hustlers.

Nick was a Greek guy who got caught with drugs on holiday in Bali. While being held on the thirteenth floor of a police station in Denpasar he tried to commit suicide by jumping through a window. Unfortunately, the glass was bullet proof and he hit it so hard that he bounced off and hurt his back, broke his hip and now can't walk properly. He was serving a 16-year sentence in Kerobokan. He didn't speak a lot of English and what he knew he learned from playing poker.

Yuki and Nori were the Japanese guys in the block. Yuki also couldn't speak a lot of English but I later found out he was a used car salesman back in Japan, as I was at home. He was stoned out of his head most nights. He called me 'Mr Por', and trying to communicate with him was like conducting a two-man comedy act each night in another language.

'How did you go with the consulate today?' I asked after he had a visit from an official. 'It brushit, brushit, brushit!' he shouted back. I couldn't help but laugh.

'What did they say to you?'

'They do nothing', he said. 'Why they come?'

'Did they give you anything?' I asked, because the consulate usually brought food or toiletries.

'One water bottle', he said, holding up a solitary finger.

'Your consulate flew all the way from Jakarta and they brought you a bottle of water?' I said. 'That's real good. I'm glad your government takes such good care of you'.

'It brushit!' he replied

Yuki lived in the Himalayas and had been in prisons all over Asia. He'd been inside an Indian jail for eighteen months and he said that was really bad. Three months later, he ended up in Hotel K which, he said, was a lot better than India.

'This is like a holiday camp', he told me with a deadpan look on his face. Kerobokan may not have been as tough as prisons in India, Thailand or even Russia, as some of the Russian inmates made clear to us, but on any given day it was its own little corner of hell.

I didn't mix much with the Indonesian inmates. Many of them didn't speak English, were high all the time or had committed such awful crimes I couldn't handle being around them.

Becky was the ugliest *benchong* transvestite you'd ever seen. She wore glasses and she had only one eye, dark brown in colour, while the glass one was a light blue colour. There was a scar on her cheek, she had acne and talked like a yapping puppy. Whether she was a man dressed as a woman or a woman dressed as a man I never found out, but she told me an interesting story. An Indonesian inmate who killed his son because he was gay ended up in Kerobokan and was placed into Block K. Unfortunately for him, Block K was where all the *benchong* are housed and they did not take too kindly to him.

That's the universe working against you big time. That's karma.

A lot of the Indonesian gang members had slash marks along their arms, showing the 'battle scars' of a hard life in the drug trade. They reminded me of the old TV show 'The Thunderbirds'—you couldn't tell what was going on behind their blank faces and cold eyes—and some were pure evil. There was never any sign of emotion on their faces.

An Indonesian we called 'Jimmy Nutjob' burned down his girlfriend's house while she was inside, and the police caught him wandering the streets nearby, badly burnt. A skinny dude, he was off his face on meth every day in Kerobokan. He'd often come out onto the tennis court when we were having a game and yell 'Me play, me play'. He'd only last two minutes because he couldn't stand still long enough to play a game. Everyone kept out of his way because he was such a loose cannon. One day, he snapped and stabbed a girl with a sword in the visiting room. He was placed in solitary confinement and then the guards found out he was planning to murder a female inmate because she owed him money for drugs. He was quickly transferred out of the prison, never to be seen by us again.

There was an Indonesian prisoner in our block who I called 'Amrozi', because he had a goatee beard and he looked like one of the Bali bombers. He was a cocky little guy I immediately took a disliking to, and after I was told why he was in prison I disliked him even more. Amrozi had murdered an Indonesian man who owed him a drug debt by giving the poor guy a 'Cheshire grin'—cutting his mouth, left and right, and ripping the top of his face off. When he was asked why he had done such a terrible thing, Amrozi said he would love to do it again, but this time to a *bule*. We stopped asking him questions after that.

Amrozi was sentenced to sixteen years but he only served eight. When he was released he went straight back into the drug trade and was caught with 3 kilograms of marijuana in Bali. Rather than come back to Kerobokan for another stint, he hanged himself in Polda Police Station. I was glad that he died and he didn't end up back with us. He was one guy the world was not going to miss.

Then there were those inmates who gambled and lost. Bashir was an Indonesian fisherman—a nondescript guy who didn't say too much. Then I heard his story. Five men went out fishing one day on a boat but only four came back. Apparently, they cut the captain up and fed him to the sharks. Bashir was sentenced to eight years but was out in four.

Bashir liked to paint and he hung his paintings up around the block. He painted one showing five balloons, four blue and one red.

'What's all this about?' I asked. Another of his paintings was of sharks. Not bad, I suppose. Interesting. Lief spoke Indonesian and talked to Bashir about his paintings. 'The five balloons represent the five men on the boat', Lief told me. He didn't have to explain the sharks to me. I got it.

It's hard to believe, but there were also a number of Indonesian children in Kerobokan. Two 14-year-old boys were in the prison with hundreds of adult males—unheard of in Western prisons—but a reality in Bali. They were keen to build up their physiques so I invited them to our gym in Block B to train.

One of the kids was jailed for crashing into a military car with his motor scooter. The poor kid didn't stop in time and his motor scooter hit the rear of the vehicle; the kid panicked when the soldiers got out of the car to inspect the damage and zoomed off on his motor scooter. The police chased him down and he was sentenced to six months in prison. The other teenager was a bag-snatcher from Kuta Beach. When he met the kid, Myu remarked, 'Hey Paul... this is the probably the kid who stole your wallet and phone, or he knows the kid who did it'.

Someone asked the kid if he ever worked his trade outside the Engine Room nightclub in Kuta. He nodded his head. Yes.

The only time the *bules* mixed with the greater prison population was outside during the day. With so many mentally disturbed people high on drugs there was always the worry that somebody would come up and stab you over an argument or some perceived slight, so I was always conscious of where everyone was in the yard. But it was when I was sleeping on the floor of the communal room that I felt my most vulnerable. I heard that gang members liked to even scores by pouring a saucepan of boiling water over their hapless victims as they slept. There were no gang members in our block, but I tended to sleep very lightly anyway.

One saving grace was that there was never the fear you might be jabbed with a needle in a shower, a horror story I'd heard about in other prisons. Because there were bathroom areas in each room I was able to shower privately, and cleanly. I cleaned our bathroom twice a week, emptying all the water and cleaning it with soap, and scrubbing the toilet and the walls. McQueen was really pedantic about the cleanliness of the room. Everything had to be perfect. His big issue was the cleanliness of the toilet. I used to clean it so well it was like a swimming pool.

Despite being surrounded by people who had committed violent crimes, there were only two people I ever fought, or came close to fighting with, in Kerobokan. I got into a 'push and shove' with Greek Nick over a game of poker, but afterwards we became good friends. I also got into a fight with a Malaysian guy who had driven everyone crazy with his behaviour.

The Malaysian was a complete fuckwit. The story goes he was detained at Denpasar Airport when he nervously changed lines and was spotted by a suspicious customs official. He was carrying drugs on his body and sent to prison. Now, in Kerobokan, he was on crystal meth and he'd lost his mind. He'd wake up in the middle of the night and do ten push-ups and then he'd just drop flat on his face, or he'd sit and stare at you for hours on end. I would be watching TV and he would grab the remote and change the channel without any warning. I was watching Motor GP one day and sipping some homemade wine with the remote control next to my leg because I wanted to watch the race. He came up and stretched out his hand out for the remote and said, 'I change!'

'No you don't, not this time', I warned him. 'You wait one hour until this is finished'. Totally ignoring me, he grabbed the remote and he changed the channel. I just lost it. I smashed him, UFC style, full on. I must have hit him eight times, and after the fight was broken up, everyone came up to me and said thank you. Even the Indonesian boss of the block came up and said, 'It's good Paul, what you did'. Finally, someone had stood up to him, and after that incident he followed me around like a lapdog.

Prison, I realised, is a lot like the outside world. There are leaders and followers, the strong and the weak and the smart and naïve.

Some people really struggled with the conditions and the rules, while others were quick to adapt. Possessions were important, but they weren't the most important thing in there and I learned to travel light and live as simply as possible. It was also important for me to stand up for myself and stand my ground when I was challenged.

The inmates of Kerobokan could spot weakness and smell fear from across the courtyard.

Outside the entrance to Block B: Billabong shorts and a blue singlet. Spot the Aussie! Note the thickness of the bars on the front doors which were locked each night at 6 p.m. by the guards.

Above: No, this inmate is not taking a bath in a water tower. He's actually cleaning out the rain storage tank because the inside of it had turned green in the humid conditions.

Below: Looking back from outside Block B to the adjoining Block A. We would walk along these paths during the day to go to the other blocks, go to the canteen or to meet in the prison yard.

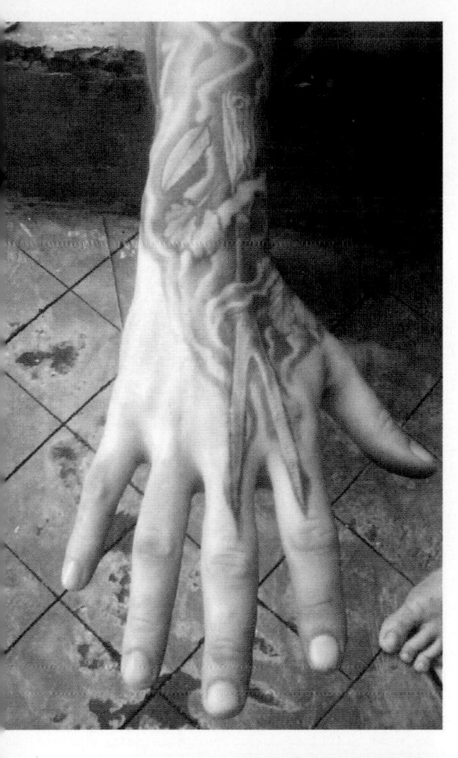

Left: A prison tattoo. Not too bad considering it is 'amateur ink' with rudimentary tools, but I easily resisted the temptation to get a prison 'stamp' while I was in there.

Below left and right: A T-shirt made inside Kerobokan prison, 'Hotel K'. The tag on the back of the T-shirt reads, 'Created in hell by people with broken lives in faith of a better future'.

Left: The front of Block B, with the newly installed water pump on display in the white box under the palm tree. The pump was purchased by a prisoner to improve the water pressure in the block.

Below: Kerobokan may have 'maximum security' but it was unlike any other jail in the world.

Right: My 'villa' (personal belongings locked in a wooden cabinet at the back of the block). Tennis balls, Vegemite and a bottle of Jack Daniels ... the diet of champions.

Below: 'Old Peter' at the bar in Block B at the start of 'happy hour' at 6 p.m. after the guards would lock us inside for the night. After the final headcount by the guards at 8 p.m. the party would start and out would come the cards, music and more alcohol.

Right: What we used as cool box to keep drinks cold in Block B . . . a plastic bucket filled with ice. The liquid in the grape juice containers is actually homemade wine.

Below: Fresh eggs being cooked for breakfast. These are not the brown eggs handed out by the prison, which were inedible, but eggs bought from outside.

One of the inmates watching a movie on his new tablet. Many of the Western prisoners had access to technology, if they weren't confiscated by the guards. Even then, all you had to do was pay a small fine to get it back.

Block B, with our modest water tank at the front of it. The green tropical gardens were just window dressing for 'Hotel K'.

CHAPTER 9

GANGS AND DRUGS

Back home in Australia in the late 1990s, I stayed with a friend I had worked with at Qantas all those years ago. I got a job at a Mercedes Benz dealership at Rose Bay and later moved to Subaru at Bankstown because it was closer to where I lived. I became very well known within the car dealership industry—I only sold quality cars and I had a good reputation as a salesman. We were the number one dealership in the country and I was selling 25 to 30 cars a month and making good money.

I met my ex-wife at Bankstown Subaru. Nicole was a receptionist there and had a six-month-old baby girl to support after her husband left her. She came from Cessnock, outside Newcastle in New South Wales, and she was keen to return home to be closer to her family. It was a whirlwind romance and after we married we moved to a little country town named Bellbird near Cessnock. I worked at a Holden dealership at Newcastle where we were sponsors of the Newcastle Knights Rugby League team when they won the NRL premiership in 2001.

I raised Nicole's daughter as my own and she remains the love of my life. Georgia is now 13 and we speak regularly. I would do anything for her. The marriage however, didn't last. Nicole was a bit younger than me and we were both on the rebound from other relationships, but we were together for three or four years and we tried hard to make it work. Nicole is a good person and I love Georgia to death. I'd like to think I was a good father to her at a time when she really needed one.

Looking back on that part of my life it was clear I was trying to please too many people. That's just the way I am. It made me feel good to help others, but I often just ended up in complicated situations that never worked out for the best.

I then met a girl in Blacktown and it was the real deal. She was a lovely Greek lady named Penny. Penny wanted children. We stayed together for four years, but whether it was my own upbringing or just my personality, I wouldn't commit to it. I wasn't ready. I had wanted to have a baby with Nicole, but it was good that we didn't. It would have been a disaster.

After I broke up with Penny, I moved to a flat in Cremorne Point belonging to the parents of a good mate of mine. We partied in Sydney for a year; the North Shore scene was quite heady, but in the end I had to walk away from that lifestyle. I was partying too hard and it was getting out of control... women, alcohol and drugs. Most weeknights I would end up at the Iguana Bar at Sydney's infamous King's Cross after a night on the town. Many of my mates in car dealerships would be out on the drink midweek (after working weekends) doing a pub-crawl through the city and I was happy to join in.

Why was I so naïve about it? I didn't know people lived like that, but I grew to like it too much and that was dangerous. That lifestyle ended up costing me a fortune and I was strung out for days on end after a big night out. I felt like I was invincible; on drugs I could drink forever and I never felt I was drunk. I just kept talking and talking, fuelled by the drugs and alcohol. I'd only start to feel it the morning after, and then it felt like I had been hit by a truck. It just smashed me.

That's why I left the city and went back to Sydney's Western

Suburbs. I was getting myself into too much trouble and wanted some peace. But soon I found myself in another toxic relationship that almost broke me.

Monica was a lovely lady. I sold a car to her and we ended up going out for a couple of months. She had a couple of kids, but her ex-husband was an unwelcome presence and they had a 12-year-old son who wasn't going to make it easy for anyone. I'd turn up to take Monica out for dinner and the kid would just give it to me. 'You're not my father; stay away from my mother. Fuck off and leave us alone'. I'd just sit there and take it, but Mon would get embarrassed and tell the kid off. One day, when it happened again, I snapped and told the kid to pull his head in. I could see his mother if I wanted to, I told him, because we were adults and he needed to keep his opinions to himself.

Well, Monica just went for me. 'How dare you speak to my son like that! Get out of my house!'

I couldn't believe it. I was trying to stick up for her. I walked out and never saw her again.

I spent the next six weeks at the gym, hitting the weights and getting supremely fit, but I had hit a wall... emotionally, physically and work-wise. I needed to clear my head and change my life, so I decided to quit my job and go to Thailand for an extended holiday. I got a good payout from the car dealership and I was cashed up and ready to kick the dust off my shoes. At the last moment, however, I changed my mind and bought a ticket to Bali.

I'd never been to Thailand before and I knew I would have a good time in Bali. It had been something of a safe haven for me in the past and was just what I needed, I told myself.

How wrong I was.

• • •

Laksa Bali is the main gang in Bali and they run Blocks C1 and C2 in Kerobokan. They run the drugs, and they intimate and kill anyone who gets in their way. On the bus to Denpasar Court, the guards didn't even handcuff the gang members, they were so respectful of them. They even let them ride the bus with their girlfriends when they were taken to court. The guards are scared of them and let them run the prison because there would be another riot if they tried to intervene in 'business'.

Baladika is the other gang that operates in Kerobokan. Sometimes the two gangs clashed and people were injured. Sometimes innocent people were injured because the gangs attacked the wrong people.

There is, of course, a pecking order with the gang bosses who are installed in jail, and most of it has to do with their reputation outside. Indonesian gang members were heavily tattooed and many wore singlets so they could show their 'muscles' after taking steroids. They were thugs. The Australians in the Bali Nine had nothing to do with gangs.

There were a lot of nationalities represented in Kerobokan: Nigerian, Malaysian, Russian, Iranian, South African, British, French, Japanese, Korean, American, German and Australian. They all had one thing in common—the drug trade. They didn't come to Bali innocent and get corrupted; they came to Bali for drugs and as part of a network of criminals. One of the inmates in prison had been smuggling drugs for over twenty years, running drugs all over the world and making millions and millions of dollars for his bosses. I don't think he lost a moment's sleep over it. Some of the drug runners in Kerobokan actually knew each other from other countries. They had partied with each other on the beach in Thailand, got high together in clubs and in hotel rooms and scored big money.

They also had another thing in common. They were all

destined to get caught. It was just a matter of where and when. Most of them were caught at the airport; there were only a couple who were arrested at their homes and rarely while out on the street. Everyone in Kerobokan said they didn't know 'the drugs were in the bag', even the guilty ones—so I never knew what the truth was. Now they had been caught, many were angry at the world. But they knew Indonesia and its laws; they knew they were risking their lives and their liberty. Why did they do it?

I never did understand. Maybe they were addicted to the drama as much as the drugs. The inmates watched themselves on Indonesian TV going to court in handcuffs and would get as excited as schoolgirls. 'Come quick, come quick', they would call out. 'Julian's on TV', and they would all come running out of their rooms to have a look. If there was a drug bust in Bali, the whole block was glued to the TV set. Everyone was fascinated by how many kilograms of drugs the people busted were carrying. 'Two kilos? Whoa!' they'd shout. 'They'll be here soon', and the jungle drum would work overtime trying to find out when they would be arriving, their nationalities and their names before they even entered the prison.

The longer I was there, however, the more I realised that I was not alone in being scammed by the Indonesian legal system and that drugs and corruption sneak into every layer of Indonesian society. When Lief was caught with drugs in Bali, he was ready to go to court and get his sentence reduced from a year and a half down to six months after giving his lawyer the money to secure it. Then his lawyer was busted for drugs. The lawyer ended up in Kerobokan and Lief lost all the money he was supposed to pay the judge to reduce his sentence. The money confiscated by the police also mysteriously 'disappeared'.

It was an eye-opener. I came into Kerobokan unaware and left with a diploma in narcotics management. I know a lot about the drug world now because the guys inside told me everything, whether I wanted to know or not.

Shabu is crystal meth, a highly addictive stimulant that gives a sense of euphoria and reduces fatigue and is smoked through a glass pipe. In 2012, several Lions Air pilots were caught doing meth and when they got busted they were thrown into Kerobokan. They were fired from their jobs, fined 300 million rupiah (33,300 dollars) each by an Indonesian court and sentenced to five years' jail.

Junkie juice is what they call methadone. Methadone was dispensed from the clinic to inmates who were registered drug addicts. Some inmates said that methadone was more addictive than heroin.

Opium is harvested in the hills of Burma, next to the Chinese border and part of the Golden Triangle with Laos and Thailand. A dark syrup is extracted from the opium pod and then taken to makeshift laboratory setups where it is soaked in vats of warm water and then dried and turned into heroin. The heroin is then distributed through different ports in China, Vietnam, Cambodia, Thailand, Pakistan, Malaysia, Hong Kong, Singapore and the state of Goa, in western India, where the Russian mafia operates their business alongside other Europeans, including Brits, and local Indians.

Sanchez, the endlessly blessing Russian, had lived in Goa, while German Hans and even Mario had also been there at one time or another so they knew the area intimately. Bali, in particular, has become the off-loading point for drugs coming into Australia, especially into Sydney, which is their biggest market.

The gangs might have run Kerobokan, but they stayed away from the *bule*s. Any conflict was usually Indonesian on Indonesian, or more like a hundred on one. Two guys were stabbed over drug debts while I was in there, and one of them died. It was later reported in Indonesian newspapers that the fight was over a pillow, but that was just a story promoted by prison officials to mask the drug problem.

The police later did a sweep of the entire prison and found knives, machetes, swords, spears, sticks, rocks and a stun gun. It's a wonder more people weren't killed inside.

The idiotic thing was that the prison itself inadvertently provided a huge number of weapons for inmates. Kerobokan was being rebuilt the entire time I was there. There was so much building material laying around the place—wood, pipe and metal off-cuts— that the gang members just helped themselves. I would walk past the canteen and see gang members buying cold drinks and rice meals with metal pipes hidden up their sleeves.

Even though as a *bule* I was fairly immune to gang violence, we'd all hear it and see it go on. I'd be out in the yard during the day and hear the click of a stun gun from the other side of the prison. The *bule*s used to sit there and wait for the sound of someone getting fried. Lief regularly talked to the gangs because he was always sourcing food through them—and he told us what they did with the stun gun. When a new inmate came in to the prison, the gangs would threaten them, hold the stun gun to their neck and give them a taste of the electricity. This intimidated the 'newby' and made it easy for the gangs to control him and shake him down if need be.

One of the Indonesian gang bosses in Kerobokan was named Bottle. He and McQueen were close friends. I only met Bottle through McQueen, but he got to know me and seemed to like me. Bottle said he respected us because we didn't do drugs and we didn't rack up bills. I seemed to get along with most of the prisoners, I think, because I was a big guy who stood out in a crowd and never caused any trouble.

Bottle regularly bought me packets of cigarettes and I would always say, 'You don't have to do that', because I didn't want to be indebted to him in any way, but then I didn't dare refuse him. I just always made sure I bought him cigarettes in return. My plan was to leave prison without owing anyone anything, not even a cigarette.

The same couldn't be said for the original guy who ran drugs out of our block. Room 4 was known as the 'Dispensary' because that's where inmates bought all their drugs. I'd see people going in and out of Room 4 all night. Not one of us in our block liked the guy who was in charge. He walked around prison with a pipe in his hand trying to act tough. He racked up huge drug debts and then he snuck out one day when he was suddenly released. Nobody knew when he was leaving and the other gangs were asking where he was. He also borrowed money from the Iranians and they were furious when they realised he had been released. They would have killed him if they could have found out where he was. He was gone!

If you weren't a gang boss, racking up debts was even more risky.

One of the Indonesians in the block ran up a 1,000-dollar drug debt—10 million rupiah, which was a lot of money in prison—and he had no hope of paying the gangs. He came up with an elaborate plan with a contact on the outside. He faked an illness by dropping to the floor and pretending to convulse and was promptly sent off to hospital. He had organised someone to drop off drugs to him in hospital, which he was going to sell to the gangs and clear his debt.

But, unfortunately for him, his friend didn't show up at the hospital before it was time for him to go back to Kerobokan. The day I left the prison, he was being given an almighty hiding.

I was never tempted to go down that track. It was dangerous to rack up credit in Kerobokan and it always seemed to be the weaker people in prison who buckled and became addicted to drugs. If you wanted them, drugs were as easy to get in Kerobokan as they were on the outside. Criminals who went in for minor larceny often came out hardened drug addicts.

Yono, a prisoner who was jailed for petty theft, was paid 200,000 rupiah a month by the prison to be the cleaner in our block. He was a good kid and I asked him what he was going to do when he got out of prison.

'I'm going into business, Mr Paul', he said.

'That's good', I told him. Work hard and save some money. 'What sort of business?'

'Illegal business', he said with a smile. *'Narkoba'*. It broke my heart when I realised that when many of the young Indonesians got out of jail they were planning on going straight into drug trafficking.

To combat the drug problem, an Australian team ran regular 'NA' (Narcotics Anonymous) meetings inside Kerobokan. I found it funny that prison officials told the world there were no drugs inside the jail. Why would they need NA meetings if drugs were not a problem? The team running the program paid inmates money for going to these meetings. Sadly, most would grab the cash and go buy drugs straight after the meeting. The drugs helped them forget where they were.

Some people were in a desperate state. One of the young guys I befriended tried to shoot up heroin in his foot and it blew up like a balloon because the needle was dirty. He was lucky he didn't lose his foot, let alone his life. He did it again before I left prison and I told him he was an idiot. He didn't care.

It was when the drugs ran out that people began to panic. When I was in Kerobokan there was a marijuana drought for five days after the latest import of grass was intercepted at the front gate. Without their weed, all the junkies couldn't function and in our block they dropped like flies. All they could do was to sleep all day because they just couldn't be motivated to do anything. When the marijuana finally came back into the prison, the place was like a Cheech and Chong movie. The whole block was just full of marijuana fog.

'Hotel K' is a real school on how to be a criminal. In most prisons, you go in to be rehabilitated. You shouldn't come out of prison needing rehab. After spending time in Kerobokan, I felt like I needed to go into rehab to get over just being there. This makes the efforts of most of the Bali Nine remarkable. Most of the guys I got to know went in as boys and are now young men. The work Andrew did with his church and Myu did in employing so many locals, is nothing short of inspiring. It's not only what they say—and I spoke to both of them—but what they achieved in prison over many years which is so amazing. Even the guards praised them. They didn't do drugs and they worked hard. They showed the world they had changed, and we hoped one day the President of Indonesia would show then clemency and revoke the death penalty. As we now know, that was not to be.

It was disappointing to see a couple of the Bali Nine guys had developed drug problems of their own and started taking methadone, but that was how they got through the night knowing they were going to wake up another day in Kerobokan. What the Bali Nine, and the other prisoners, need is counselling, real counselling, so they at least have a chance at a decent life when they finally get out.

If they get out.

CHAPTER 10

REMEMBERING THE BALI BOMBINGS

Until 2012 I loved Bali, and so do the over 8 million tourists who flock to Indonesia every year. There is so much to do that most people really do see it as a paradise, and the fact that it all comes at a fraction of the price of a Western holiday makes it seem too good to be true... and it is.

Depending on your interests, there's surfing, rafting, hiking, biking, elephant rides, animals parks, fun parks, shopping, numerous restaurants and bars for eating and drinking or just relaxing by a resort pool. A trip there can be anything you want it to be—a relaxing holiday, an experience in another world or a fun time exploring the nightlife and meeting lots of new people. I tended to drift to the latter option.

Bali is rich in culture and I always found the Balinese people to be gentle and friendly. Although is only between 5,000 and 6,000 square kilometers in area, it is home to more than 4 million people. The religion of the majority of inhabitants is Hindu, with Muslim, Christian and Buddhist faiths also represented.

There are temples, lush tropical gardens, rice fields and other plantations, remote beaches, neighbouring islands and even two active volcanoes to visit—Mount Agung and Mount Batur—if you are adventurous enough. Transport is cheap so it's relatively easy to travel around the island and you really need to get out of Kuta, Seminyak and Legian, which are tourist traps, if you want to experience the beauty of the island.

The downside of Bali is the insane and dangerous traffic, the narrow roads, the hawkers and scammers, and the filth and poverty in the streets—the tourist revenue doesn't seem to benefit ordinary Indonesians. The Balinese people are wonderful, but many Indonesians and immigrants from Thailand, Borneo and India have come down to Bali to try and eke out a living and make a buck or two out of unsuspecting tourists. There is also a lot of rubbish in the street; the smell of blocked drains tends to overpower the whiff of incessantly burning incense or the many frangipani trees that dot the place.

Since the Bali bombings began just over a decade ago, the Department of Foreign Affairs (DFAT) has regularly posted travel warnings about potential terrorist attacks, militant groups, public venues under bomb threats and even natural disasters such as tsunamis. And still, people flock to the Island paradise.

The truth remains that despite its many flaws, it's very easy to fall in love with a place like Bali. I know I did.

• • •

The Bali bombings—the first in October 2002 when 202 people were killed, and then again in 2005, at the cost of another 20 lives—still cast a dark shadow over Kerobokan when I was imprisoned there a decade later. When Kuta's Sari Club and Paddy's Pub were bombed on the night of October 12, 2002, I was back living in Australia and the tragedy shocked the entire country. Having been to Bali so many times and enjoyed many evenings at those nightspots with both friends and strangers from overseas, I was devastated. I had hung out at Coogee and Maroubra, in

Sydney's Eastern Suburbs, and drank with mates like the young men and women who lost their lives in that bombing.

I could only imagine the terror and destruction the night that claimed all those lives.

About eleven o'clock on a busy Saturday in October 2002, a suicide bomber carrying a backpack entered Paddy's Pub and detonated a bomb on the dance floor. This caused many patrons to evacuate onto the street as the dying and injured reeled from the initial blast. Seconds later, a white Mitsubishi van packed with over a tonne of explosives outside the nearby Sari club, was remotely detonated by mobile phone, immediately killing a second suicide bomber who parked it there. A third bomb was detonated outside the American consulate in Denpasar, causing some damage but fortunately only minor injuries.

The blast and engulfing fireball was catastrophic. The car bomb, which comprised potassium chlorate, aluminum powder, sulphur and a TNT booster packed in plastic filing cabinets, destroyed the two clubs and the surrounding residential and commercial district. The local hospital was overwhelmed by the numbers of the injured, and many Australian victims were flown home still suffering the effects of their serious burns. Eighty-eight Australians lost their lives—the most of any country—along with innocent tourists from the United Kingdom (27), the US (7) and countries from almost every other continent. Just as importantly, 38 Indonesians were killed in the blast, many of them local Balinese. The bombers were indiscriminate in causing as much damage and death as humanly possible.

Why?

The organisation suspected of planning the bombing was an Indonesian Islamist group called Jemaah Islamiyah. Headed by cleric Abu Bakar Bashir, young Muslims in Indonesia were easily radicalised by Bashir's rhetoric in light of the September 11 attacks the previous year and America's impending invasion of Afghanistan and Iraq. There is no doubt the Bali bombers received help in sourcing, buying and then making the explosive devices from al-Qaeda, but the active ringleaders involved in the Kuta Beach bombings were quickly rounded up by Indonesian police who were able to track the terrorists' mobile phone activities leading up, and especially after the event.

Although more than thirty people suspected of playing an active role in the bombing were sent to an already crowded Kerobokan prison, Amrozi bin Haji Nurhasyim and his older brother Ali Ghufron (also known as Mukhlas)—were sentenced to death in 2003 after Amrozi's younger brother, Ali Imron, turned prosecution witness in exchange for life in prison. Imam Samudra (also known as Abdul Aziz) was also sentenced to death and a fifth 'ringleader' named Mubarok was later sentenced to life in prison in Jakarta.

Abu Bakar Bashir was jailed for two and a half years for 'conspiracy to commit treason', but the conviction was overturned on appeal following his release from prison in 2006.

I was told by some of the long-serving prisoners that the arrival of the terrorists at Kerobokan caused quite a commotion—media, helicopters, police with guns drawn and riot squads to keep the crowds back. Prison authorities renovated a tower building which previously housed gardening equipment, a library and a 'VIP' cell to house the Bali bombers in maximum security. The three terrorists, especially Amrozi, became celebrities in Kerobokan years before Schapelle Corby and the Bali Nine arrived there. The smiling assassin Amrozi, who gave a 'thumbs up' in the courtroom when they handed down his death sentence, especially infuriated the families of his victims by smiling at a willing Indonesian media and chanting pro-Islamic slogans.

Because many innocent Balinese and Indonesian locals were killed in the blasts, there was tension both inside and outside the prison. While Balinese protesters demonstrated outside the prison, the Indonesians inside Kerobokan yelled, 'Kill Amrozi! Death to the Bali bombers!' Many threw stones at the tower block trying to strike Amrozi who was kept in the front cell. Other prisoners, however, and not all of them Muslims, became infatuated with the terrorists and would listen to their rants and go to the canteen and buy provisions for them. Even some of the Muslim guards came under their spell, growing 'goatee' beards in solidarity with them.

The attitude of some of the police who arrested the Bali bombers was disgraceful. They shook Amrozi's hand in front of the cameras and appeared happy at the media attention. The terrorists had no remorse for any of the people they murdered or maimed.

The fear was that the Bali bombers were still able to influence their followers from prison. Members of the Bali Nine, who arrived in Kerobokan in 2005, told me that they had heard prisoners yelling out to the terrorists *'Bali bom lagi!'*... 'Bomb Bali again!'

On October 1, 2005, triple suicide blasts in Kuta and Jimbaran killed 20 people including four Australians. The three Bali bombers were questioned in Kerobokan, and it is believed Samudra was involved in recruiting the three suicide bombers for this second attack. Abu Bakar Bashir, who was in prison at the time, stated that 'God' was talking to the Indonesian government through these actions. Although released, he was later jailed in 2011 for inciting terrorism and financing a terrorist cell.

None of the Australians in Kerobokan had any time for the terrorists. One of the younger guys allegedly asked the prison guards to give him 30 minutes with Amrozi to 'beat the shit out of him'. I don't know if that was false bravado or not, but I'm glad I didn't have to deal with them in prison. I talked to the boys about it and none of them were comfortable with the fact that they were living in the same cells as terrorists who killed so many Australians.

One of the *bule*s in Block B remembered a conversation he had with one of the bombers. 'Why you in prison?' Iman Samudra asked. 'Drugs', the *bule* said. 'Hashish!' he replied, 'Oh, hashish no good... it bad for people's lives', the bomber added.

'Hang on!' the *bule* said. 'You murdered more than 200 innocent people. Where the fuck do you get off giving me morality lessons?' Samudra became angry at this and refused to speak to him.

As the third anniversary of the first Bali bombings approached in the weeks after this second attack, tensions in Bali heightened as the local economy took another hit. Demonstrations outside Kerobokan turned violent and the riot police were deployed. The decision had already been made to transfer the three terrorists out to Batu Prison on a remote island called Nusa Kambangan off the coast of Java.

Their appeals all but exhausted, and with no hope of

remissions or rehabilitation, Amrozi, Mukhlas and Samudra were secreted away from the prying eyes of the media to a prison regarded as Indonesia's 'Alcatraz'.

As soon as the Bali bombers left Kerobokan, the Bali Nine became the 'poster boys' of Kerobokan for the Indonesian and international media. Having talked to all of them about this, I know they resisted the temptation to play up to the media because of the gravity of their situation. Andrew Chan was an extrovert and could handle the media well enough, but Myu was an introvert and the others, including Renae, struggled with the media attention. They have real trust issues—at times with each other and with the media—and told me of the time a television cameraman deliberately started a fight, was arrested and spent three months in Kerobokan trying to suck up to them for an 'exclusive interview'.

After he was arrested, Scotty Rush refused to allow the media to snap a clear picture of him. The press even misidentified his image, publishing pictures of Matty instead, which drew a wry smile from him. When the prison guards called him Kerobokan's 'movie star' and taunted him that he looked just like 'Leonardo DiCaprio', Scotty stopped exercising, put on weight and cut his hair. He wasn't up for the whole media circus. He refused to treat Schapelle Corby as a celebrity, taking great delight in calling her 'Corby' when the rest of the world referred to her by her Christian name as they do Madonna, Rihanna or Kylie.

In 2008, the Bali Nine watched the news of the executions of the Bali bombers on Indonesian television. Perversely, this finally made the prospect of their own fates very real to them.

In the early hours of 9 November, the three terrorists were woken before dawn, handcuffed to prison officers and driven to an isolated beach. The Indonesian death penalty regulations outlined on the Internet provides an insight into what happened to them: 'Once arriving at the place of their death', *Penetapan Presiden No.2* (1964) states, 'the condemned is blindfolded, although they can choose not to be. The condemned is given the freedom to choose how they will die—standing, sitting or lying'.

A white apron with a round red target over the heart was draped over each of the terrorists.

Thirty-two soldiers of the Indonesian Mobile Brigade who passed 'appropriate psychological tests' made up the firing squad of three sets of twelve. Some were issued blanks, some live rounds. 'If after the shooting, the condemned still shows signs they are not yet dead, the Commander immediately gives the order to the head of the firing squad to let off a *tembakan pengakhir* (finishing shot) by pressing the barrel of the gun against the temple of the condemned, right above their ear'.

The three Bali Bombers were executed simultaneously, but it is unknown whether a 'finishing shot' was required. No outsiders can witness an execution in Indonesia... no family, no friends, no media.

This was the fate awaiting Lindsay Sandiford, my friends Andrew and Myu of the Bali Nine and other prisoners on death row in Kerobokan. It seems incongruous that regardless of how heinous and ill-conceived their crimes in the drug trade, they could be dealt with in the same manner as terrorists who killed so many innocent people.

When I was in Bali in 2012 I visited the memorial on

the site of the destroyed Paddy's Pub in Legian Street, Kuta Beach. A large marble plaque set in carved stone lists the names and nationalities of the 202 victims. The national flags of the victims flank either side. I shook my head in disbelief. So many lives taken, for what?

I was in Kerobokan Prison on October 12, 2012, which was the 10th anniversary of the first Bali bombing. The mood was subdued and the prison guards quiet and respectful. They marked the anniversary by giving the prisoners extra rations of food.

CHAPTER 11

SWEATING LIKE A CORNERED NUN

I wanted my seasons back. I wanted a cool autumn breeze and a crisp spring day. I wanted a winter. I was sick of the relentless heat and the 30+ degrees nights. Then there were the insects, the mosquitoes and flying ants that buzzed and bit you and crawled over your skin at night.

It was hot as hell inside. There was not one night, except when I got sick and was shivering with a fever, that I even needed a blanket over me. There was no circulation of fresh air in the block, just the still stench of sweet. I never got used to that. I wanted cool, cold air. That's what I missed.

I loved it when it rained at night because of the noise of the rain bouncing off the metal roof. It was something different. On the other hand, conditions inside worsened when it rained. It was so humid in our block that the room would steam up. Then the roof would start leaking and I couldn't move my mattress anywhere to lie down without getting dripped on. Two of the drug dealers in the block actually paid the prison 500 dollars to fix the roof and it still kept on leaking.

Kerobokan was its own microclimate. It was far hotter and more humid than the outside and it was always a topic of conversation among inmates. Two of the Brits were talking about it on one occasion. 'I'm sweating like a dolphin,' said the first guy and we all laughed. 'Hot?' the other replied. 'I'm sweating like a cornered nun'. We had to laugh. It was a pathetic situation.

Because I sweated so much, my sheets were drenched each night and I would have to hang them out every day to dry and wash them every two or three days.

Ali, the emaciated Iranian, often complained it was too hot. He told the big boss in Block A that he didn't like the smell we made when we cooked our food. Then we were told we had to cook outside. 'How can we cook outside when you lock us in at six o'clock?' we complained. Cooking food didn't make conditions any hotter and the Iranians didn't help themselves, playing ping pong outside in the heat all day. It was absurd.

As time went on I started to feel that the prison guards used the heat to play mind games with us. If you asked a guard something, the answer would invariably be 'Maybe, maybe not...' It drove me crazy. Then they would often turn the electricity off for no reason. We had three ceiling fans in our block and one day we counted 27 times that they turned the electricity off. When the fans stopped, we were sweltering. The power cut out at least ten times at night. I would often be in the shower when they turned the electricity off and suddenly everything would go black and because there were no fans running, I would be drenched in sweat all over again. The guards said they were trying to fix the electricity, but there seemed to be no urgency to fix anything. The fans would be broken for two days at a time, but then *everything* was broken in Kerobokan. When the electricity went off, the pump stopped and there was no water available. It was a punishment—the Indonesian justice system, or whatever evil force was working inside Kerobokan, making life a misery.

As one of the 'lifers' remarked, if you wished for wings to fly out of here you'd receive a broken pair.

As well as the power cutting out every day, there were loose wires everywhere that gave you a nasty shock if you trod on them. I received electric shocks twice in Kerobokan. I tried to boil some water in a broken kettle and I couldn't get the plug to work.

I dropped the kettle in the water tank while I was standing in the bath and it gave me a nice jolt. My arm was sore for a couple of days. The second time I was shocked I pushed bread into the toaster too forcefully and got a shock through the bread!

We had an electrician in Kerobokan, an inmate who was called upon to fix appliances, but he was utterly useless. There was an electrical transformer box on the outside of the canteen and one day it just blew up. Smoke was billowing out of the box, so we wandered over to see what was going on. Standing there in his blue work overalls was our trusty electrician holding an electrical chord in his hand. I don't know if he'd tried to plug it in and then blew it up or if he had pulled out the wrong wire, but the look on his face was priceless. All the guards were running around like chickens with their heads cut off and this poor guy was standing there just looking at the chord in his hand.

I had my own run-in with the electrician during my time in Kerobokan. Another inmate had given me a fan but I needed an extension chord to run it to where I slept so I could keep cool at night. I bought a brand-new 20-metre extension chord from another inmate but it wasn't working so I gave it to the electrician to fix. He said he would bring it back the next day but when it came I couldn't find him anywhere. When I finally tracked him down I demanded my chord back and he handed it over. I didn't really take much notice of it until I plugged it in. The chord had changed from a white colour to a creamy yellow; there were now only two plug sockets instead of four and it was now only 10 metres in length.

I went back to him and told him it wasn't the same chord, and he said; 'Your one broken, you take this one'. I suspect he probably cut it down and made four chords out of it.

My friend Virginia bought a kettle for me. It was a plastic kettle she had bought at a local shop, but when I filled it up with water and plugged it in, water started leaking down the chord and it wouldn't turn on. I told her it didn't work and asked her to take it back but when she tried the store wouldn't refund her money. That would be right. If there is anything you can't sell in your own country because it's either faulty, too dangerous or it's downright illegal, send it to Indonesia and someone will try to sell it.

Perhaps that's why they had a philosophy class inside the prison—to teach us to accept what we knew we couldn't change. The classes were run by a lecturer from Belgium who worked at the university in Denpasar. He ran the philosophy class for ten weeks and we all went along for a while. After a few weeks it all became too much for my head; it was digging too deep into me and I had to stop going. I wasn't ready then for that much soul-searching and introspection.

Drawing class was more my thing. An Australian lady named Lizzy Love ran the drawing class at Kerobokan. She loved all of the guys who came along and we enjoyed it. Drawing class was a far better option than some of the other activities, like the compulsory aerobics. Every Friday, six inmates from the women's block would come in all dressed up in their Lycra and do a choreographed dance that the whole of Indonesia did, copying an aerobics class on TV. One block would have to go on alternate Friday mornings at 8 a.m. and do aerobics. It was mandatory. You had to go otherwise you had to pay a 10,000 rupiah fine, which is only 1 dollar. I went most of the time because it was something different, but sometimes I paid the 10,000 rupiah and slept in.

There was also a church, a mosque and other temples within the prison grounds. The church was a neat little wooden chapel— an open area with plastic chairs on either side of an aisle. Church sessions were every afternoon and Andrew would read a passage from the Bible. Every Sunday, someone came in from outside the prison to conduct the service. The mosque was brand new and beautifully detailed in white tile.

I was skeptical that many people who found themselves in prison turned to God. The Nigerians in our block always thought God was going to save them. They never paid for their room and the Indonesians kept asking them when they were going to pay their rent. 'Don't worry', they told the gangs, 'The Lord will provide. Jesus will come and he will help me'. It was their solution to everything.

My faith was pretty much non-existent when I went into prison. Following my mum's heart attack, however,

I reconnected with church and I even went along to the services in Kerobokan for a couple of Sundays. The mass was in Indonesian and I didn't understand a word. At the end of the service we would shake hands with each other. All the girls would get dressed up, and after months of living cheek to cheek with just men, it was also good to sit behind them and have a sneaky look.

When you went to church in Kerobokan you had to write your name in a ledger before going inside. Going to church added to your remissions and you were also fed well. Most people wouldn't actually sit through a service, but when the book came out they'd just turn up, sign it, and grab their food and leave. We would be given a pyramid pack of rice with some meat. We later found it out that it was dog meat.

'What's wrong with these people?' I complained. I so was disgusted. Mickey said not to worry about it. The locals eat dog meat all the time.

I never ate a meal at church again.

Andrew Chan formed a church group that used to meet regularly outside the tower block. He really tried his best to gain some meaning from being in prison and help others to come to terms with it as well and find some inner peace. I went along sometimes to listen and talk with him. We were sitting in a group under a tree, talking about life in general, when a fight broke out in the courtyard. 'A fight! We're off!' was the call and everyone immediately ran over to watch the fight, leaving only me and Andrew sitting under the tree.

So much for finding spiritual meaning in prison.

After a while I sat Andrew down and said I didn't want to go to church anymore. 'I can't shake hands with child molesters, rapists and murderers', I told him, having discovered what crimes some of the Indonesians had been jailed for. Looking back on it, I had no problem shaking hands and becoming friends with drug smugglers, but that was the line I drew in Kerobokan... a very wobbly, faint line in the sand.

Andrew said he understood my decision. He respected the fact that I came up to him and told him that going to church wasn't for me. It was the right thing to do, he said, rather than trying to fake my way through my sentence and become one of those people who just came for the free food and remissions.

The Indonesian gangs certainly had no respect for church. While one service was on, they came in and grabbed a guy who owed them money and forced him to the ground. They then burned his eyeball with a cigarette. If someone had shown that level of disrespect inside the mosque it would have started a serious internal war.

There was nothing to do at night in Kerobokan except watch terrible Indonesian TV, so we would just sit around playing cards, chatting and drinking. We would start drinking outside in the afternoon and then take all our contraband indoors after the guards locked us in for the night. When the guards came back at eight o'clock to do the final head count for the day, we would hide it from sight and then produce it as soon as they were gone. The guards would let us know we were coming by banging wooden sticks on the bars outside our block.

We played poker every second night and there were some big stakes. The gangs were involved with drugs and even some of the *bules* ran their businesses from inside the prison, so there was a ready supply of cash available. I won

250 dollars one night, but then lost it the next time round. I wasn't that interested in the high stakes games. Dice games were also popular, especially with the Indonesians, but you lost your money twice as quick. For those who didn't have any money, there was always a game of monopoly. Alcohol was also readily available, if you had the money. The guards would do an alcohol run to the 'Circle K' convenience store across the road from the prison and sell it to us at inflated prices. They would also smuggle in bags of *arak*, a local brew, and sell it to prisoners. A beer costs about 3 dollars but they were too hard to bring into the prison in bulk. A little bottle of vodka, which cost about 18 dollars, was the beverage of choice. It was in a proper vodka bottle but the quality of the alcohol was questionable. We suspected a lot of it was homemade hooch. Sometimes, we got a good batch; sometimes it tasted like rocket fuel. One batch was so bad, the Brits in our block joked it must have been siphoned from the fuel tanks of the recent Lion Airways crash at Denpasar airport.

The Indonesian gangs tried to get in on the act and bought alcohol from the guards to sell on to us. The plan was make us pay even more for it. But they ended up throwing a huge party in their block, drank it all themselves and got wasted. That's how hopeless they were. They couldn't even be bothered to walk out of their block to sell it.

CHAPTER 12

VISITORS

I came into Kerobokan with the clothes on my back and ended up with everything I needed. When I was arrested, the police confiscated my luggage and didn't give anything back. All I was left with was two pairs of shorts, one T-shirt and one pair of underwear for 58 days at Kuta Police Station. I washed my clothes every second day and gave up wearing underwear. All I wore were shorts because it was so hot I couldn't wear anything else.

People both in prison and from the outside were very generous and donated things to me. McQueen gave me some T-shirts and a couple of Australians visiting asked me if I needed anything. The article that broke the news of my imprisonment carried a photo of me in a blue singlet that was sent to me by Emma, a girl I know from Australia. McQueen mentioned to me one day that he wouldn't mind wearing a blue singlet because it was bound to be cooler in the steamy conditions and 'typically Australian' attire. I asked Emma if she could send me over a couple—one for me and one for McQueen— two working-class boys from Sydney's wild west!

Visitors to the prison brought in food and other prison 'luxuries' such as toothpaste, soap, talcum powder, laundry powder, moisturiser, Dettol, Band-Aids, cotton buds and mosquito coils for prisoners. Some even brought money as gifts. Some of the visitors also brought in chocolates but they would melt almost immediately if you didn't put them on ice.

The visitors' room in Kerobokan is a concrete courtyard with adjoining visiting rooms. Official visiting hours were from 9 a.m. to midday, and 1 p.m. to 4.30 p.m. on Monday to Friday, and 9 a.m. to 12.30 p.m. on Saturday and Sunday. Visits were only meant to last 15 minutes, but could go on for hours. It cost 5,000 rupiah for visitors to enter the visitors' area, 10,000 if you wanted to sit on a mat.

The prison guards regulated the visitors' room and it really depended on their mood on the day as to whether you'd be able to see your visitors or not. During one of his regular visits, Ronnie tried to come in to give me the money my brother wired me. I was trying to get through the front door and a fat guard had his foot in the way. I said I had a visitor and he said no I didn't. He wouldn't let me open the door. The other guard said, 'You come back. Come back later'.

'No', I demanded. 'My friend's coming in. I need to see him'. I was standing just outside the visiting room. I saw the big guard shift a little bit and I went back in and pushed the door open. I walked straight through without waiting and I was finally able to see Ronnie.

There were always fights in the visitors' section, including the occasional stabbing. On one occasion, Lief was sitting in there talking to a girl, and her Indonesian boyfriend came in and hit her from behind, knocking her out. It was crazy.

He was upset that Lief was talking to her. We'd talk to all the girls in there while we waited for our own visitors to come. I didn't want anything to do with the local Indonesian girls who came to visit the prisoners because all they wanted was money. They would talk to a *bule* and be all nice and sweet and then their Indonesian boyfriend would get jealous and want to start a fight.

I got used to the sight of people discreetly having sex in the visiting room. I would look around at the mass of people sitting on the floor and ask myself, 'are those people doing it over there?' They may have been under a blanket or have had a female friend sitting on their lap, but it didn't leave much to the imagination. It happened all the time. There was no such thing as conjugal visits in Kerobokan but the guards would turn a blind eye... to a point. An Indonesian girl was caught having sex in the church toilet and she was promptly transferred out of the prison. But Kerobokan was not an equal opportunity prison. Nothing happened to the guy she was with.

I had no family members visit me because I told my brother not to. One of my mates from Subaru came over and tried to see me, but he was turned away. Also, my mate 'Puss' found out that I was in Kerobokan and he flew over to visit me. The guards wanted to charge him $400 AUD to see me and then they turned him away. I was furious when I found out through another friend on Facebook. Nevertheless, it was good to know that people still cared about me.

Although I didn't receive many visitors in Kerobokan, some of the other Western prisoners regularly received visitors and sometimes I got to know them too.

The girlfriend of Bali Nine Michael took a shining to me

because I was talking to him and trying to help him through a difficult situation and she brought me a lot of things: board shorts, a couple of shirts, toothpaste, anything I needed. You couldn't get anything if you didn't ask. I ended up asking visitors, strangers, anyone, if they could get things for me and they were only too happy to oblige.

The higher profile prisoners tended to receive many more visitors than those who were less well known. A quiet little schoolteacher came to visit Lindsay in prison and fell in love with a Ugandan prisoner from our block. Suddenly she was flying out to Bali every holiday and buying all these things for her new boyfriend. I also heard she was planning on getting a map of Africa tattooed on her back. I thought this was fucking unbelievable! I could never understand how you could form a relationship with someone in prison—until it happened to me too.

Michelle was a friend of a lady who I first met when she was visiting the Bali Nine a couple of months before the end of my time in Kerobokan. The next day, Michelle came to the prison again and I struck up a conversation with her. Michelle was in Bali for a week and came to the prison almost every day, which should have sent alarm bells ringing for me then and there. I had seen for myself how some women—local Indonesians on the make, visiting Westerners romanticising life behind bars and the desperate and lonely—came to Kerobokan with stars in their eyes.

Michelle asked if I needed anything, but she had already brought in so much fruit I couldn't eat it all before it all went off. 'You don't have to do that', I told her when she arrived with bags of fruit in both hands, and I ended up giving most of it away. She asked for my phone number and we started talking. It was good to have someone to talk to because I was sick of talking to the guys in prison. It was nice to talk to a woman for a change. She kept bringing me cigarettes and I was starting to eat really well. I felt guilty because I was milking it a little, but I was in prison and I wasn't making her do it.

At the end of her week in Bali, Michelle had to return to Australia but within weeks she was back to see me again. I was flattered by the attention but I was in no position to think about the future or work on a potential relationship. She started sending me bizarre messages romanticising the situation. 'You're the most amazing person', she gushed. No I wasn't. She said I had the best attitude of anyone in prison. Did I? That was a little more overwhelming than normal. She spoke to me from Australia, which I really appreciated, and told me she would be 'there for me' when I got out.

I didn't realise Michelle was speaking literally. She was physically there waiting for me outside Kerobokan when I was eventually released midway through 2013.

CHAPTER 13

CHRISTMAS IN KEROBOKAN

Each year, an Australian businessman who owns a hotel in Bali organises a Christmas party for all the Australians in Kerobokan. It's a wonderful gesture and it's something that everyone really looks forward to as it breaks the monotony of prison life. There were 15 Aussies in prison when I was there in 2012.

When we got together in one of the visitors' rooms a couple of days before Christmas, there was food and drink and a present for each of us neatly wrapped and placed on a table. We drew names out of a hat before we were invited to select and open a present of our choice. However, if someone else wanted that present the rule was that they could come up to you and ask for it. If someone claimed your present, you could go and choose another one. I suppose it was an interesting way to foster the spirit of giving at Christmas time. It was also a lot of fun, and a great way to get the conversation started.

One of the presents was a small safety box with a lock and fifty Australian dollars inside. I ended up with it, but only after I swapped with Renae Lawrence. Scotty Rush then claimed it off me. Eventually, it ended up with someone else. I received a toiletries pack, but Malcolm claimed that and I finished with a small stool, which was okay by me. It was all good fun.

I found myself sitting next to Malcolm and across from Renae Lawrence and Schapelle Corby at the Christmas party. I had met Renae a couple of times through the other members of the Bali Nine, but it was the first time I had the opportunity to talk to Schapelle.

She was such a high profile prisoner in the adjacent women's section of Kerobokan that she didn't mix with the general prison population. She was allegedly given high levels of medication to help her with her 'depression and psychosis'. When she talked, she talked so softly it was almost inaudible, but other than 'Hello' and 'Merry Christmas' we didn't have too much to talk about anyway.

The real gift at the Christmas party was being allowed to stay up late enough to see the stars at night. Usually we were locked in our prison cells by 6.30 p.m. At night, you could stand at the front entrance which had been locked and search a patch of the sky for the moon and the stars. While looking, I discovered that there are no shooting stars in the Indonesian sky to wish upon. If there are, I certainly didn't see any during my time in Kerobokan.

The following day, Schapelle spotted me in the canteen and asked if I had used any of the stuff in the toiletries pack. I was so taken aback by this unsolicited conversation that I didn't have the heart to tell her that Malcolm had the toiletries pack, not me.

'No, I haven't, thanks," I said.

One of the Nigerians in my block was trying to chat her up and I just leaned over and said, 'Merry Christmas for tomorrow, Schapelle'.

'You too', she replied in a whisper.

I saw Schapelle a couple of times in the visitors' section after that, and I used to say hello to her sister Mercedes, but we never had a conversation and I have no real insight into her life in prison—or whether she was innocent or guilty. She reminded me of a fragile doll that could break at any moment.

Schapelle has always maintained she knew nothing about the drugs inside the bodyboard case, but the sheer weight should have alerted her something was not right. Given her emotional state when she sentenced to 20 years, you couldn't help but feel that she thought she was going to be found innocent. Some would say it was because she wasn't coping with the fact that she had been caught in the first place.

There has been a lot of conjecture over the years about her mental state in prison, and this has led to her eventual parole in her tenth year in Kerobokan. The only insight I have to offer is that even doing ten years in Kerobokan would be like serving double in an Australian prison.

Schapelle has done her time and I wish her nothing but good luck and peace of mind.

Enjoying a Christmas party and receiving a modest gift didn't go down too well with the other inmates in our block. There was no party organised for the other *bule*s, and the sight of us coming back after a meal and drink, and with a present no less, was bound to be met with some resentment.

We must have celebrated too much at the Christmas party, because the prison guards cancelled our New Year's

Eve party. We were informed by the prison authorities there would be no drinking allowed on New Year's Eve. There were drugs all through the prison; people were tripping out on LSD or magic mushrooms and smoking weed until they were stoned blind but we couldn't drink alcohol?

What kind of decision was that?

We'd planned the party weeks in advance and had already bought all the grog we needed. The other problem was that by the time they made the announcement we were already blind drunk.

Weeks earlier, an inmate named Marco had made 16 litres of wine so that it would be ready for the party. Previously, Mario had made wine from grape juice by adding raw sugar to it to make it ferment and he had it ready to drink in a week. It tasted really good. But Marco, a proud Frenchman, said he could improve on that. The Brits bought all the ingredients Marco needed and got some of their Indonesian 'gofers' to bring it into the prison. Marco filled up a huge water cooler full of his concoction and we paid 100,000 rupiah for a litre. We started drinking at three o'clock in the afternoon and listened to music until we were locked inside and the announcement was made that the New Year's party was banned by the guards. We were all wasted. We emptied all the booze into water bottles—Scotch was poured into a dark-blue bottle, vodka in a clear bottle—and sat round pretending we were drinking water. The chief prison guard took one look at us and commented, 'Very good. No one is drinking', despite the fact that we were all falling over drunk right in front of him.

The Iranians also went into the liquor business in readiness for New Years, but theirs was a less successful venture. They had imported a quantity of vodka—or what the Indonesians passed off as vodka—and were selling it in two container sizes. 'How much is a small container?' I asked. They told me it was 180,000 rupiah. The next day I went back but by then they only had the big containers left. 'How much is that one?' I enquired. 180,000 rupiah they said. I couldn't believe they were selling both containers at the same price. What was the point of selling it if they weren't going to make any money? I told Mario and he tried to explain it to them too. They still didn't get it. The Iranians weren't cut out to be business people, I guess... just drug addicts.

After the guards left at eight o'clock, we brought out the rest of the alcohol that we had secreted around our block and tried to kick-start the party. But we had been drinking all day and our enthusiasm started to waver. No one could agree on which music to play anyway so the party was over before it started.

CHAPTER 14

GROUNDHOG DAY

For a prison that held over 1000 inmates and was three times fuller than it should have been, Kerobokan could be a very lonely place. At times I thought I was losing all my senses as well as my sanity. As soon as I thought I was making a little progress I'd get belted backwards. I came into prison weighing 110 kilograms and left at 85 kilograms spread over my 6 foot (1.82m) frame. I was physically fit and trained every day, but at the end of it my eyeballs felt as if they were sinking into my head and the energy was being sucked out of me.

Blue, the colour of the prison guard uniforms, stopped being a colour for me. For me, the guards were just dark shapes to be avoided. German Peter came up to me one day when he obviously saw that I was struggling and said to me, 'Don't sell yourself to the abyss, Paul. It won't pay'.

At the time I shook my head and dismissed these words of wisdom as the product of another of Peter's drug hazes. But upon reflection, it may have been the best piece of advice I received in there... and Peter was perfect proof of what happens when you do sell yourself to the abyss.

I felt I was wasting away, and I was only in there for ten months. It was as if there was something evil under the prison, like a giant magnet. Some days I would struggle to get up off the ground as if something was anchoring me to the concrete. Many people struggled to sleep on the concrete because it was so hard on your body.

Sleeping on a mat on the concrete played havoc with your bones and many of the inmates complained of 'rhino skin'—hardened calluses that developed on their back from lying on the ground, day after day, month after month and, in many cases, year after year.

Prison drained me of my energy, affected my diet and interrupted my sleep. I smoked two packs of cigarettes a day in prison, which didn't help. I quit smoking as soon as I left Bali and haven't wanted a cigarette since.

There was also the constant fear of being deliberately drugged by the prison establishment. We discussed it quite a lot. Were the authorities drugging us to make us docile, to reduce our libido or shut down our minds? Mickey thought as much and he refused to eat the food; he either bought food in or had it freshly made in front of him. If you pissed someone off in Kerobokan, it would be so easy for them to get back at you by poisoning you. It got to the point where I didn't accept food from anyone.

I could also sense my memory going. After a couple of months I found I couldn't remember names, movies, and even the names of friends. 'This is bullshit', I said to myself. 'Why can't I remember anything?' I would start to Google something and then realise that I couldn't remember what the hell it was I was Googling.

The lack of stimulus was draining the life out of me.

CHAPTER 14

Doing time in Kerobokan was like living in a parallel dimension, an alternate reality where everything was upside down and nothing functioned the way it should have. It was like the movie, 'Groundhog Day', repeating the same mind-numbing monotony of prison life every day.

One inmate pointed out to me that we all actually paid money to go to Kerobokan. 'You're paying off the lawyers and the police and the entire justice system and you still end up in prison'. When I thought about it, he was right. All the bribes and kickbacks are to ensure you spend less time in jail, but they don't do anything to stop you from going there. I was relieved, when I heard that, that I hadn't given more than 50 dollars of my brother's money to Sara or the police.

The lethargy and misery in Kerobokan was all-consuming. Some people used drugs to escape from it, others gambled away what little money they had. But, for me, one of the things that got me through was music. Strangely, when I first arrived there I would do anything I could to avoid listening to the songs people were playing around me. I didn't want to listen because didn't want to be reminded of happier times in my life on the outside. I wanted to steel myself, be strong and get through the sentence in a vacuum, without losing my mind. Australian music was the worst. I hated hearing songs that reminded me of home: Daddy Cool's *Eagle Rock*, Guns and Roses, Metallica, or anything by ACDC.

But after I while, I realised I needed music. A song would play and it would make me happy as soon as I heard it. Soon I started downloading music onto my iPhone until I had over a hundred songs stored on my playlist. We also had access to an iPod dock where we played songs out the back of the outside area, and it felt great. I'd sing along with the other

Western Sydney boys to the music that reminded us all of home and I'd forget where I was for a while.

I even had a go at rapping to the music.

It's not a war being fought offshore
No one coming to save the day
They're the ones committing the crime
Just time ticking away

• • •

I would be listening to music and on an absolute high, and then the power would cut out and I'd be back down in the dumps again. It was total emotional rollercoaster. I was sitting out the back of our block one day and I was playing Alicia Keys' version of 'New York State of Mind' on my iPhone. Alberto the mafia boss came up to me with a serious look on his face and said, 'Paul, that is my favourite song'. I was shit scared there for a moment.

One night, Mickey and I were sitting inside their room drinking wine and I put on Frank Sinatra. 'This is unbelievable', Alberto said. He loved it.

Many things could be done to help the mental and physical health of the prisoners in Kerobokan... if anyone in authority gave a fuck. A pet dog would have made all the difference. 'Just give me a blue cattle dog and I'll be happy', McQueen admitted and even Scotty Rush's eyes lit up.

One day, the head of the prison brought in his golden retriever and he had it at the tennis courts where we were playing. I walked straight up to him and started patting him and rubbing his belly. It made my day. He stunk a bit but I didn't care, I just enjoyed playing with him. All the Indonesians were standing there just looking at me. They didn't like dogs at all and couldn't understand why I would want to play with him and let him lick me. I threw a ball for the dog to fetch and the poor animal just looked at me with his big brown eyes. I guess no one had ever played with this dog.

Something as small as patting a dog lifted my spirits so much.

To have had a dog there the whole time would have made a huge difference to my state of mind. It would have given me something to care for and given me a sense of purpose, something to stop me feeling sorry for myself and losing my grip on reality. A companion that was unconditional in its affection—a mate who would never let you down. Prison officials actually told us they were going to run a dog program where inmates could care and interact with a pet dog, but the Muslim inmates complained you couldn't have dogs too close to the mosque, so it never happened.

We never stopped trying to improve conditions inside. The Australian consulate organised for the drug Xanax to be available to inmates to treat anxiety and depression, but they wouldn't provide vitamins or protein shakes to help with our diet and nutrition.

Some of the Bali Nine told me the consulate agreed to do it and then reneged on the plan.

For every step we took towards improving our living standards, there would invariably be something outside our control to push us back.

CHAPTER 15

THE MEDIA

This is the original news report, published on May 1, 2013 on Australian news site ninemsn.com that alerted the world to my story:

It started as a relaxing three-month holiday in Bali for Sydney man Paul Conibeer, after he quit his job as a car salesman and headed off on a solo overseas adventure.

One year on, Mr Conibeer now spends his nights on a mattress on the floor of Indonesia's notorious Kerobokan prison, drifting in and out of sleep as cockroaches and rats scuttle over him.

'A snake crawled into our cell the other night and we had to kill that', Mr Conibeer tells ninemsn from inside Kerobokan.

'It's the heat that's really unbearable'.

'When you're inside a locked cell with the heat of 55 bodies, you are constantly sweating'.

Mr Conibeer says it was a 'comedy of errors' that landed him where he is today. The 44-year-old, from Blacktown in Sydney's northwest, was arrested in Bali last August because he was unable to pay his hotel bill after being robbed.

He claims he ended up in prison because he refused to pay bribes to local authorities after his arrest.

At first he tried to organise for his family to send money to pay his bill, but claims he became frustrated each day as he was told the amount he owed had increased.

The amount he owed rose from $3000 to $9500 in just three weeks, he says. In October, he was jailed for one year after failing to pay up.

The trouble started around August 27 on a night out in Kuta, Bali's popular party district. Mr Conibeer was pick-pocketed outside a nightclub and lost everything – his money, bank cards and phone, which had all his contacts stored in it.

He also had no travel insurance, so he had no hope of getting any of it back.

He couldn't access his savings because his bank would only send a new ATM card to his home address in Australia.

The next day, he was asked to check out of his hotel and explained to the owner that he was unable to pay his bill on the spot.

'I asked if we could go down to the police station so I could report it', he says.

'But when we got there, they suddenly put handcuffs on me and said, "This bloke is charging you, because you owe him money".'

'They wouldn't say what I'd been charged with. They just said to me, "You're a criminal now".'

Mr Conibeer was locked in a dark police cell for 60 days with no mattress or pillow and no access to a phone.

'I had nothing, not even a pen or paper', he says.

'And they wouldn't let me use the Internet so I couldn't get in touch with anyone or access my bank account'.

Mr Conibeer, who was born in New Zealand but has lived in Australia as a permanent resident since he was a child, says he was given 16 days to pay his hotel bill.

He was not initially told how much he owed, but he expected the bill for the two week stay to come to around $1300.

Police contacted the New Zealand Embassy the day after his arrest but Mr Conibeer was told consular officials could do little more than get in touch with his family.

He was not allowed to contact the Australian Consulate-General because he had travelled to Bali on a New Zealand passport.

Three days after his arrest, Mr Conibeer talked a police officer into letting him use Facebook to retrieve the contact details of his mother and brother in the US.

I asked the police officer how much I owed, so I knew how much money to ask them to send', he says.

'He said, "You need to pay $3000 within 16 days to get out of jail plus give money to the Chief of Police upstairs and deal with Immigration".'

But two days later, Mr Conibeer claims he was visited by a woman appointed as his translator, who told him the amount he owed had changed.

'The translator told me the policeman was wrong and I actually had to pay $5000 within six days to get out of jail', he says.

'My mum is on the pension and my brother isn't working, so they didn't have the cash but my brother organised an unsecured loan of $5000 to get me out'.

But he claims his translator soon told him the $5000 would no longer be enough – the debt had risen to $5500 and this amount was not guaranteed to get him out of jail.

According to Mr Conibeer, the debt continued to rise over the next three weeks until he eventually stopped trying to pay it.

He claims it peaked at $9500 [sic] after his translator learned his brother was organising a loan of $20,000 against his mother's house, to pay for his release, airfare and to help him get back on his feet.

'I didn't pay the money because I believed it wasn't going to go to the hotel. I believed it wasn't going to go to the appropriate people. It was going to line someone else's pockets'.

Mr Conibeer represented himself in court and was sentenced to one year in prison after refusing to pay the debt.

In Kerobokan, he shares a cell with 55 international prisoners, including members of the Bali Nine.

Conditions are filthy, food is in short supply and illness spreads quickly, he says.

'You cough up shit like you've never seen before in your life'.

But it's not as bad as he expected. Prisoners are well treated and he stays fit and sociable.

Mr Conibeer says he would rather do the time than spend his money paying off local authorities.

His greatest frustration with his situation is that he receives no support from the Australian government in jail, despite being a permanent resident.

'I lived in Australia my whole life and paid taxes there, I've never lived in New Zealand', he says.

The Department of Foreign Affairs and Trade told ninemsn Mr Conibeer was not receiving consular assistance from Australia because he was a New Zealand citizen.

A spokesman for the New Zealand Ministry of Foreign Affairs and Trade said the embassy had provided Mr Conibeer with support and information but was unable

to pay hotel bills, fines, bail or get New Zealand citizens released from prison.

Police in Bali refused to comment on Mr Conibeer's claims over the phone.

• • •

Back in Australia, my friend Greg Sanderson called Channel

9 journalist and newsreader Peter Overton and told him that an Aussie named Paul Conibeer was locked inside Kerobokan Prison alongside the Bali Nine. A journalist from Ninemsn, the website used by Channel 9 news, contacted the Australian consulate in Jakarta and they confirmed I was in prison, but I corrected them by telling them I was a Kiwi. They got my phone contacts from the New Zealand consulate and a journalist later called me in prison.

Channel 9 was very interested in doing a story on me, they said, but could I send them some material I had gathered on my phone? I had been documenting everything—photos, audio, video and lots of information about diverse characters and bizarre events that I had witnessed inside. It was unbelievable footage, they said, can we do an interview with you? I did the interview over the phone with journalist Fiona Willan in late April, 2013.

National Nine News journalist Mark Burrows then contacted me by text. He said he would like to come over and interview me, along with Andrew and Myu from the Bali Nine. Mark had organised through their lawyers to come in and do some interviews with them and it would be the first time television cameras would be allowed into Kerobokan. Mark came in and interviewed Andrew and Myu, and ran their stories on Channel 9 news program, 'A Current Affair'. My story made it into mainstream news services, but it was heavily edited and broadcast only the basic facts of my situation.

It was Andrew Chan who first told me I was in the news. A Google search brought up Fiona's long article about me on Ninemsn. When some of the *bules* asked if I had talked to the press, I told them that I hadn't, and that my brother must have contacted them. I didn't know how the other prisoners would react to my story finally being published. It was later to prove a prophetic move.

The extended interview with Mark Burrows never went to air. Then Denham Hitchcock, Channel 9's US-based international correspondent contacted me. He wanted to do a documentary on the dark side of Bali—the drugs, the murders, the rapes and especially, conditions inside Kerobokan. Would I tell my story to him? I told him I had already done an interview with Channel 9 and I wasn't even sure if it had aired. Denham said it hadn't and that Channel 9 wanted to save the details of my story for the documentary. What payment was I looking for, he asked.

It's a dangerous thing to ask someone sitting in a third-world prison to place a value on their story. A million Australian dollars? A million rupiah? A McDonalds meal? I knew what my freedom was worth—everything I owned—but I had no idea what my particular story was worth. I decided to talk to them and worry about the details later.

Denham and producer Hamish Thomson came over to film the documentary 'Bali: The Dark Side of Paradise' in May 2013. When Denham came into Kerobokan, the prison guards knew I didn't usually have visitors and sent out another prisoner named Paul to speak to him. This Paul did not take kindly to Denham's outstretched hands and introduction.

'Who are you?' the other Paul asked.

'I'm from Channel 9 in Sydney', Denham told him.

'I don't talk to the media. Fuck off', was his terse reply. Sometime later, they called for me to go to the visitors' room, but by then our block was aware that I was talking to the media. Denham was an open, friendly young guy. 'Mate', he said. 'I heard about your case and I can't believe what's happened to you. It there anything I can do?' It was fantastic just to have someone to talk to. We didn't even do an interview; we just sat and talked about rugby league, surfing and other things young blokes might talk about in a pub or a bar... life, love and lost opportunities. We just talked and talked.

We agreed to do an interview after I was due to be released from prison in June. Denham bought me a memory card for my phone and I used it to get the photos and film Channel 9 could use for their documentary. I had enough of my material for a documentary of my own, but it was all ruined by a virus and it only left me a matter of weeks before my release to gather all the information I needed.

While Denham was visiting me, he experienced first-hand what goes on inside Kerobokan. He was standing outside the jail, taking photos of the prison, when a brick flew over the wall from inside the prison and almost hit him. He picked it up and noticed there was sticky tape around it, securing a small package on one side. All of a sudden an Indonesian male pulled up on a motorbike and said the package was his and to give it to him. Denham was happy to oblige. Someone was selling drugs from *inside* the prison to the outside world.

Denham became a good mate, and he got his documentary made.

He has allowed me to reproduce the article he wrote after visiting me in Kerobokan Prison. Thanks DH.

• • •

The guards at Bali's feared Kerobokan prison look at me with only mild interest, the only white man in a huddled group of chattering visitors with a plastic bag full of groceries at my feet. The air is humid as only Bali can be. Sweat a constant companion, along with a few nerves. I'm about to go and meet a man who I've never met, who doesn't know I'm coming. A man who has quite a story to tell.

I got here a few weeks ago to shoot a documentary.

Stepping off the plane is an experience in itself. A prickle of sweat confirms my arrival as I'm drowned in close to one hundred per cent humidity and stifling heat. Long queues of bored passengers, customs as basic as it gets. You have a passport and money, and Bali wants you to use both.

It's by far Australia's favourite holiday destination. Close to one million of us are expected to file through Denpasar airport this year, battle the hectic traffic and the street hawkers, and stand on those magnificent beaches framed by waves that every surfer dreams of. Hotels can be cheap, beer is even cheaper, and everything and anything can be bought on the street.

But we are not alone in our love of this place. When you add domestic tourists with international, Bali is flooded yearly with eight million people, a number that's twice its population. Many feel that a growing desperation for the tourist dollar, fuelled by the chasm of disparity between the Rupiah and just about any other currency, has changed a place with a reputation of being one of the friendliest destinations on earth.

Consider this. In 2012 an Australian died in Bali every nine days. That's almost one a week. A lot of it is from misadventure like motorbike accidents, or drug overdoses, but there is also a long list of murders. Add to this the number of assaults, rapes, and robberies, and Bali has a dark side that's not advertised in the brochures.

You know the big names, but it might surprise you to find out there are close to 20 Australians behind the razor wire at Kerobokan prison, otherwise known as Hotel K, although it's unlike any hotel I've ever been to.

CHAPTER 15

After more than two hours, finally the guard at the gate yells out my number in Bahasa and an Indonesian woman next to me shoves me forward, I head through the metal door and into a small room packed with guards, I hand over the grubby plastic card with my number on it, and my mobile phone. Two of them start rummage through my bag of groceries. I ask them about their day, but no one responds. Another man pats me down and sends me on my way with a toothy grin.

The visitor's area is nothing but a square concrete floor with a corrugated iron roof. The temperature is stifling, and not helped by the number of people inside. Visitors mixing with inmates, who come and go as they please. The men with wives and girlfriends try and take the corners and the walls. Larger groups get pushed to the middle.

There are reed mats if you're lucky. The concentrated noise of people talking is deafening. I can make out some members of the Bali Nine. Andrew Chan is sitting in a prayer circle holding hands.

I palm some rupiah to one of the guards. 'Paul' I say. 'Aussie Paul'. 'He's a friend of mine'. It's some time before a confused face appears. He looks in better shape than I thought he'd be. Friendly, a little weather beaten, wary. I shake his hand, we sit down on the concrete and I explain why I'm here.

Paul Conibeer's case defies belief. He's just spent one year in Kerobokan prison, eating handfuls of rice at meal times, and bunking down shoulder to shoulder with hundreds of Indonesians on concrete floors, for what amounts to an unpaid hotel bill in Kuta.

A dispute over that bill, led to police involvement, and once he was in custody he claims police demanded bribe money to release him, a figure that escalated to a point where he simply couldn't pay. He took a chance on the legal system, and it came down hard. One year in Kerobokan.

Using a smuggled mobile phone Paul has documented his time behind the walls. The drugs, the weapons, the wild parties, the brutal enforcement of prison rules. The men murdered before his eyes.

Previously the only look inside these walls has been stage managed by prison guards. Painting, dancing, family time. Paul's account, backed up by photos and video, is the real 'Hotel K'... a look behind the scenes through the eyes of an Australian inmate just trying to survive. It is, at times, hard to comprehend that such a place exists.

Don't get me wrong. As a keen surfer I love Indonesia.

I have travelled there more than half a dozen times ... Bali, Nusa Lembongan, Lombok, Sumbawa, Sumatra, Nias. It's a beautiful place with beautiful people. And the documentary that airs this Sunday tells the whole story of the place they call the island of the gods, not just the dangers. And Australians are not totally blameless either. You only need to spend a few days in Kuta to realise that drunk and out of control Aussies are contributing to the problem. The Balinese are generally a gentle people with a spiritual and religious culture. Marauding groups of loud obnoxious boozed up Aussies don't help their opinion of us and could be partly responsible for what appears to be a growing malevolence towards us.

What is certain is the statistics and numbers don't lie. It's become a dangerous place for travelling Australians. Murders and rapes that go unsolved, assaults and robberies that leave people disfigured and scarred. A place where magic mushrooms and speed are perfectly legal, but a justice system that will sentence you to 20 years jail for a bag of weed. A place where, like it or not, police corruption is part of the system, and Australian authorities have very little influence. This, despite an increase in the money we give them, to well over 600 million dollars a year.

It's long been our playground, our favourite holiday destination, but have we loved this place too much? To me it's still paradise, it's just that now, I see a lot more than the surf and the palm trees.

CHAPTER 16

THE RAID

We got word that the Indonesian police were going to raid Kerobokan three days before the scheduled hit. We were told they were flying down from Jakarta on the Friday at lunchtime and they were definitely coming in to raid the prison on Monday, but we didn't know which block. We knew they wouldn't raid the blocks run by the gangs, because that's how the riot started in February 2012. So, we thought it might the *bule*s' turn and all the Westerners in Kerobokan started packing up all their phones, cameras, iPods, iPads, DVDs and CDs to hide them so they wouldn't be confiscated by the police. Then there was the illegal contraband in the block... the alcohol, the drugs and the money.

The guards already knew we had all of it. One member of the Bali Nine even carried his new plasma TV past all the guards in order to hide it. He didn't even bother to put a towel over it to cover it up; he just walked straight out into the open and hid his TV in the workshop so that the police couldn't find it.

Our entire block decided to hide all of our contraband

in the ceiling. Then we realised that all our valuables were in the one place. If someone told the police and they found it, then we were going to lose everything, so we went back to hiding our belongings individually.

Monday came and went and nothing happened. Perhaps the rumours weren't true? Two weeks passed. We had taken all of our contraband out of hiding and we had almost forgotten all about it when the raid finally happened. It took us completely by surprise. It was 5.30 in the morning and everyone was asleep when the police came into the room, guns drawn and yelling orders in Indonesian. They went from room to room, hurrying the sleepy prisoners to stand outside. Then they started the search.

The police found phones, laptops and drugs, with the gang boss in charge of Room 4 furious he lost his stash. We didn't have enough time to hide our phones. I had two phones—one, an old phone that I used to speak to my brother and mother—was in my pocket. I had another phone with Internet access that was in the cell with McQueen because he used to go on the Internet at night when I went to sleep.

The police went straight to McQueen's room and grabbed my phone; it was as if they knew it was there all along.

After the raid, the police left the prison and the guards came in and gave us a big speech. If we were caught with drugs, they said, we would lose any remissions (time off our sentence) we had earned, which was useless because most of the prisoners who controlled the drugs were already on life sentences. They weren't eligible for remissions. If we were caught with drugs, the guards warned us, we would be taken back to court to be sentenced again. Hang on! We all thought. If you're a lifer, what are they going to do to you?

Give you double life? No one believed a word the guards were saying.

The amazing contradiction was that although the prison guards confiscated our phones, months earlier they had addressed all the blocks individually and told us that to top-up our contraband phones we had to buy our phone credit from them at the front office. The cards cost about 100,000 rupiah and the phone credit lasted for quite a while.

The prison wanted to corner the phone card business. They even put a telephone booth in the canteen where you could register your phone card on your phone. All this in a place where phones were not allowed! When I was in the canteen and I saw the 'Dr Who-like' tardis, I couldn't help but laugh at the absurdity of it all. You could use your phone in full view of the guards in the designated area of the canteen, all while not being allowed to have a phone.

The raid was first reported in the Indonesian newspapers.

The media came out the next day and they took photos of all the contraband that had been confiscated... *almost* all the contraband. It was reported in the paper that there were no drugs or alcohol found in the prison. They had to be kidding. The guards confiscated all the drugs from the block and then it all mysteriously disappeared. The authorities then went on national TV with the same story.

No drugs or alcohol, just phones, they proudly announced. It was laughable.

They displayed the confiscated laptops, phones, DVD players and the odd knife on a large table and encouraged the media to film it. It was funny because we then saw all of our possessions on the Indonesian news and pointed at the TV saying, 'Look, there's my phone, there's my laptop'.

The reality was that everyone felt down after the raid because we had lost contact with the outside world—contact with our family and friends, the news and the Internet. It crushed us. The ability to connect with the outside world is often the only thing that keeps people alive in prison—the hope you have after talking to your

family. Everyone pleaded with the guards, 'Please, please, I need my phone', but realistically, the guards were never going to give them back. We were being punished.

Afterwards, the rumour quickly spread around the prison that the raid was all because of me. I had spoken to an Australian reporter, and the rumour was that the reporter had gone to the house of the police chief to interview him about my case. The story being readily circulated was that the reporter let slip that the Westerners in the prison had phones and that they communicated with the press. The police chief contacted Jakarta and his superior ordered the raid on the prison. It gets better. Apparently, the prison officials met with the Jakarta police who were going to raid the prison on the Monday and talked them out of it. It was almost as if the prison guards met the police at the front door and said listen, you know you can't raid the prison because there will be a riot and we don't need that right now. Let us get the prison ready for you.

The story concluded that the Jakarta riot police went out for the night and were entertained by hookers as a 'pay off'.

Then they came back a fortnight later anyway.

Unfortunately for me, the rest of the block just assumed that because Denham came and asked for me, that I was the one who had caused the raid. I was responsible for everyone losing their things and so the threats started to come thick and fast. 'Either you replace everyone's phones and computers, or you're dead', was the general gist of it. Mario led the doubters, but conceded to wait and find out the truth first before going any further with it.

Thanks for the vote of confidence.

Worried, I texted Denham on a borrowed phone from one of the Bali Nine. 'Please tell me you didn't go and talk to this prison guard, because I'm in trouble here'. No, he said. He told me he wouldn't be doing any stories on me until I got back home to Australia. That's all I needed to know. 'I trust you', I told him, 'but these pelicans in here are paranoid. They're all going off'.

I gave the other inmates my explanation. 'I've already done a story and it's on the Channel 9 website, and I showed you all that weeks ago. Remember?' At the time I showed them, they were all happy for me and had all laughed. 'Oh man, you're going to be famous in Australia!' I reiterated to them, 'That's the only story I've done. I haven't done another story and I never gave an interview to a reporter'.

During the day I sat by myself because no one would talk or associate with me. Up until that day I was everyone's best friend and then all of a sudden no one wanted to know me. It was a lonely feeling in prison, let me tell you. I couldn't sleep because I thought I'd be attacked in the middle of the night... or worse. Even McQueen was a bit distant. He didn't want to commit himself to any one side, and all he said to me was, 'If that's your story, then back yourself'.

Finally, Greek Nick said he believed me. He was the first to break ranks, then one the Iranians named Masud came up and said, 'It's alright Paul, don't worry'. Masud was a gentle giant, and easily the biggest guy in the prison. His brother Said was also in prison and one by one the Iranians came around.

'We know it wasn't you who told the police, Paul', Said offered.

The issue died down, but I couldn't even look Mario in the face after that. And I got no apology from him either. Not even a hint of a 'sorry Paul' for almost getting me killed in prison.

Who tipped Jakarta off? There was a special task force inside the prison that monitored the phones of the big drug bosses. That's why the big bosses used as many as eight sim cards at a time to try and throw the police off track. The raid was mainly to curb the drug trade inside Kerobokan... the drug trade that, according to the prison guards, didn't even exist.

The guards then decided to collect the fingerprints of the entire prison, but our block didn't want to do it because obviously no one wanted their fingerprints to be on file. Eventually, they forced us so we had no choice. A lot of the prison records were burned in the February 2012 riot, so the rumour mill was working hard again saying the authorities had no proof who was even inside Kerobokan. People started coming up with grand ideas. 'If they don't know I'm in here, then they won't know I've escaped', some said.

'What are you talking about?' I replied. 'Just Google yourself and there's a picture of you in a bright orange jumpsuit. You're on the internet!' They had no idea.

After the raid some inmates also became upset with Linga, the boss of our block, because he should have warned us that we were being raided. He said that he didn't know anything about the raid so he couldn't have warned us. 'You still had your phone on you', we told him, 'You could have texted us'. After that, we always checked that the door of our block was locked in case we got raided during the night. That's what was so bizarre about the raid. Two padlocks were placed on the door every night by the guards, and yet no one heard the police coming. Surely we would have heard them opening the padlocks.

Before the raid, our block was known as the laziest in the prison. We slept in and got up whenever we wanted because we were *bule*s. We weren't regimented like the rest of the prison. The guards said we had no respect for them, which was true. When they come in the morning and we were still sleeping when they tried to do a roll call, we'd go back to sleep for a while or put our hand up while lying on the ground. All the other blocks were up at six in the morning and they'd have to have the floors washed by eight. Our cleaner, Yono, said that in other blocks, if inmates didn't get up they got a bucket of water poured over them. After the raid, however, the guards came down hard on our block. All of a sudden, we had to be up at six every morning to clean, and a big fat guard would come in and kick everyone's feet to rustle us up. 'You should be standing up at the door', they said. 'Show some respect'.

Fuck you.

Most of the guards inside were useless, but not cruel. The prison guards earn a small salary by Western standards so they're open to corruption. Most of the guards treated us okay. Without them we couldn't get anything into the prison and then we would be really up against it.

There were a couple, however, I couldn't stand. One of the head guards would come into our block and if we didn't stand up he'd kick us, or kick over our water bottles, and then laugh. He was a fat heap and he'd have his shirt hanging out. Nobody liked him.

After the raid, the prison guards made us all line up outside our block for a good old lecture in front of the local media. 'There are no drugs in Kerobokan', the fat guard waffled on in front of a compliant media. 'There are no computers and no phones in the prison'. We all laughed at that. 'This is a good prison', he continued, 'and we all get along like a big family'. The guard loved the sound of own voice and we were lined up for an hour in the heat. Prisoners were dropping like flies.

The next day, an Indonesian escaped from the prison. They were still rebuilding the back section of the prison wall that had been damaged in the riot and a young Indonesian dug under the corner of a concrete slab as soon as the blocks were unlocked in the morning. When the police caught him, they sent him back to Kerobokan and the guards brutalised him. Escaping from prison was a huge show of disrespect to the gang boss who ran his block and the prison guards who put the gang boss into power.

They broke the guy's feet with a brick and then transferred him to another prison.

It was impossible to respect the guards. They demanded our respect with one hand and in the other quite happily took bribes and bought us alcohol. One of the most bizarre incidents that I witnessed was during the celebrations for the prison's 49th birthday. The gangs inside the prison paid for a party as a thank you to the guards. They hired six prostitutes to dance on a small stage and supplied the guards with drugs and alcohol. A guard went into our block, smoked some crystal meth and came out and danced on stage with the hookers. He was off his face. Lief took the video of the celebrations on his phone and he sent it to me later to use in the documentary footage I gave to Channel 9.

Denham Hitchcock gave me the money for a new phone and a family member of one of the Bali Nine bought it for me. The worst thing was that I had a lot of photos on the memory card that was in my confiscated phone and I needed them for my documentary. I kept on telling the guards in the weeks leading up to my release that I didn't want my phone back—they could keep the unit. I just wanted the sim card from it. I needed the sim card because it had phone numbers I needed to contact my consulate so I could get back to Australia. I also needed the memory card on the phone, but I wasn't going to tell them that.

I went to see the prison chief before I was due to leave Kerobokan. 'I think about it', was all he said. 'You come back and see me the day you leave'.

The guards turned a blind eye to a lot of things, but I still had to be careful. After the raid, I was looking at my new phone while I waited to get a haircut at the Block B barber. An Indonesian guy was sitting there under the barber's gown getting his hair cut. He must be a new bloke, I thought, because I hadn't seen him around the prison and he looked like a pretty big guy. I decided to take a photo of the barber for the documentary I was gathering for Denham. I calmly took the photo. A few minutes later the guy took his gown off to reveal his uniform underneath. He was a prison guard—not just any prison guard but the new second in charge of the whole prison.

Luckily, my phone was on silent and it didn't make a noise as I took the photo, so he didn't hear it, or he just ignored me. I could easily have been busted and had my phone confiscated again. I never told anyone in the block because everyone was on edge after the big raid. I couldn't go back to the block and say I had just taken a photo of the prison second in command getting his hair cut because I would have been beaten up for being so stupid.

CHAPTER 17

THE BARELY-LEGAL SURF SCHOOL

I realised certain inmates had been set up by the police because they were 'non-users' caught with small amounts of drugs. The police set up people with small amounts of cocaine, heroin or weed because they couldn't afford to plant huge amounts of drugs on them. A couple of grams worth was all they could afford. But those who were set up could still be put away for years even for small amounts.

Julien was a very cool surfer guy from the south of France and one of the first people I met when I arrived in Kerobokan Prison. Along with David, a Spanish guy, they shared a similar fate. They were both set up with drugs. Jules was set up by his Indonesian girlfriend and David by a business partner who wanted to rip him off.

Jules ran a surf school in the south of France. He worked for three months of the year in France and that funded his lifestyle for the rest of the year in Bali. When we asked him who his students were, he said mainly 16-year-old schoolgirls. One of the Brits in our block christened it the 'Barely-legal Surf School'. We all laughed, but Jules protested, saying no, no, it wasn't like that at all. It was his business and he wanted no trouble with the law. That would come to him in Bali.

Jules leased a home in Bali for two years at a time and lived the high-life before returning to another Northern Hemisphere summer in France. He had an Indonesian girlfriend and they lived together and shared a bank security box because it was difficult for internationals to open and operate bank accounts in Bali.

Jules had just come back to Bali from France in September 2012 when a friend told him that he had seen his girlfriend with another guy at a wedding. At first he didn't believe him, but the guy showed him photos from the wedding and the two of them were all over each other. Jules confronted his girlfriend about it all and it didn't end well. He threw her out of his house and threatened to change his bank deposit box, leaving her with nothing.

I'll let Jules tell his own story. He sent me this email from France and he asked that I publish it in this book:

> My name is Julien Bouzats. I was detained in Bali from the 10 October 2012 to 18 February 2013. If you Google my name, you'll find the following media report:
>
> *'Bali expat set up in drug case; French Citizen and resident in Bali for eight years. Detained by police 4 months and 8 days after 0.05g of heroin was planted in his helmet (by the police).'*
>
> I spent the afternoon on Kuta beach while my motorbike was parked outside in the street with my helmet on it. At the end of the day I took my motorbike and drove home. On the way I stopped in a Circle K supermarket to buy

some drinks. When I got in the shop a guy with black leather jacket stopped me and showed me a police card with the words *Narkoba Bali*. "We want to search your bags and other items because we think you have drugs on you'. They asked me to follow them outside because he didn't want to search me in the shop.

I followed him outside where seven other 'black jacket guys' were also waiting for me. When I passed the door, the other guys surrounded me. Then the first guy turned back to me with his hand already in the helmet and pulled out a small packet with brown powder inside. At this point, the nightmare started.

It was amazing. They immediately found what they wanted before they even started searching! Then they told me: 'So, now we will search your bag, motorbike and house, and you have to stay with us during the research' But they already 'got' me! They just wanted to stick to the procedure! I understand later these 'undercover police' are street junky gangsters, who are willing to make some money and get a promotion by arranging to trap innocent people with drugs.

The police spent two hours searching my house, pushing me to say that the 'packet' belonged to me. I ended up in a filthy 9 metre square cell at Polda Police Station in Denpasar. I stayed there alone for six days, with no contact with anyone on the outside. I then stayed another seven days, along with nine guys sleeping on the floor in 35-degree heat. Infested with mosquitos, with no windows or fan with minimal light. A hole in the floor, known as a 'Turkish toilet' and a bucket of brown water served as a bathroom, with just enough food to survive.

Some days, we had nothing to eat for 24 hours.

Every day, I dealt with investigators and my lawyer to prove my innocence. None of my fingerprints were on the packet, but police don't use fingerprint evidence in narcotics cases. My blood and urine tests were negative but the police didn't care. They were waiting for the money. I was done. The police made a fake report saying they followed me for a week and saw me buying drugs on the beach every day. Local workers on the beach said that I did not buy anything, but the police didn't want to hear from those witnesses. If the police report was right, why don't they also stop the dealer I was meeting? That's because there was no dealer.

A ten-year-old child would not even believe this story! The police investigation did not follow the normal protocol but then nothing was logical in this country. I soon realised I was dealing with a well organised, corrupted system … a lucrative business where gangsters, police, investigators, lawyers, labs, doctors, judges, prosecutors and interpreters are all in on it. Of course, the police and justice system in Bali would not give up the chance to make some easy money for the sake of freeing an innocent man, and yet all the 'clues' pointed to my innocence and the set up being perpetrated.

I was sure to be found guilty of possessing 0.05 gram of heroin, which had been planted in my helmet by the police. My lawyer gave me three options:

Pay $100,000 US and go free.

Keep my urine and blood tests negatives, be charged as a drug dealer with a penalty of between 4 to 12 years in jail.

Paying $35,000 US to change the tests results to positive, and then I'd be charged as a drug user with a penalty of 4 to 12 months in jail.

I chose the third solution, which cost me $35,000 dollars to pay the gangster undercover police, police chiefs, investigators, the police lab to change results, the doctor, my lawyer, the prosecutor, and the five judges who heard my case as well as the immigration department.

Justice is money in Indonesia. I was finally sentenced to 4 months and 8 days after going to court six times in court over a 4 months period. After I served the remainder of my sentence in Kerobokan, I was to be deported and blacklisted by the Indonesian government for a year before I could come back into the country.

I spent two months in Polda Police Station in Denpasar, locked away in two different cells with 45 other guys locked in almost total darkness, 24 hours a day and 7 days a week in inhuman conditions. We were treated like animals, with rats and cockroaches running over our sweaty bodies while we tried to sleep on the dirty floor. There were two Turkish toilets and two dirty brown water bins for 45 people. There was a dark green slippery carpet of mushrooms on the floor because of the humidity and the fact that the "bathroom" had never been cleaned. We had to hang onto the walls and walk slowly as not to slip over and fall.

Each day, prisoners suffered fever and sickness, but the guards didn't care and they refused to supply medicines. For food, we had 200g of rice and two bite- sized pieces of omelettes with fish or chicken each day. On some days, we could buy local food from outside the jail but guards charged double the price and often ate your food or kept your money.

After that, I was transferred to Kerobokan, an overcrowded jail without security guards on the inside and corrupt guards willing to turn a blind eye to illegal activity … as long as they were paid off. Twelve blocks, with numerous cells managed by prisoners and drug traffickers and gang law. 'Hotel K' has its own infamous reputation. It was a total mess.

Justice is money in Indonesia, especially in Bali.

Every paradise has a piece of hell and people should be aware of that. Don't expect any humanity there if you find yourself in trouble either, because the Balinese justice system is the most corrupt institution in the world when they have decided to 'take you down'.

Whether you're innocent or not, you have to pay or you'll end up in jail for years and years and the judges have no remorse in destroying life.

How did this happen to me? I later received information that my Indonesian girlfriend was at the origin of the plot with the help of gangsters, undercover police and the corrupt Balinese justice system. After my last time in court, the prosecutor said to me: 'Hey Julien. Just choose a better girlfriend next time. Take care now, because if your ex-girlfriend does this to you again you'll get twice the sentence and it will cost you twice the price!'

And then the guy just smiled at me. He got his part of the money. This kind of trap happens every day in Bali in different ways.

After almost a decade of happiness living in and travelling to in Bali, it all ended with a snap of a finger. I have so much to say about Kerobokan. I'm so happy Paul is writing this book.

Never trust and never forget... you're the '*bule*'!

Julien Bouzats.

Julien's lawyer tried to scam him out of another 12,000 euros so he would get his pre-sentence period of four months. If he didn't pay, Jules was told, he could get another two months added to his sentence. 'What should I do?' he asked me, 'I have no money left?'

This is where my own experience with the Indonesian justice system came into play and Dave's words came out of my mouth. 'Tell them to fuck off', I told him. 'It's a scam'. He had already completed three months, so he only had another month to go. 'What's another two months anyway?' I said.

Jules called their bluff and he refused to pay any extra money. He was sentenced to the original four months after just a couple of minutes before the judge. When he was finally released, however, immigration officials held him for two extra weeks because he didn't pay them off. He was supposed to fly to Thailand, but he didn't make the flight.

Jules was the first prisoner who showed me how to undo my handcuffs on the bus to court. I was waiting for him to come back from court one day and he came in holding his loose handcuffs. Where the fuck did you get those? I asked him. He said he had just undone them on the bus back from the court. Some of the Indonesians on the bus showed him how to pick the locks with a toothpick—the handcuffs they used were absolutely ancient. There weren't any police on the bus and only two guards at the front in the driver's section. I saw it myself whenever I had to go to court. The prisoners would undo their cuffs, sit unchained for the whole bus ride and when they got to court they would just put them back on.

Jules later took his handcuffs back to France as a souvenir.

Jules's friends from France came to visit him and later sent him baguette rolls with fresh ham and cheese. They dropped it off at the front door and they asked the guards to give it to Jules, also stuffing 5 million Rupiah in the bag for him.

Jules saw the rolls but not the rolls of money. 'Paul, I can't eat all of this', he said as he tucked into the food. 'Do you want some?'

We demolished the rolls and then he wrapped everything up and threw the paper bags in the bin. A little later, he came back in a panic and said, 'Paul! Where's that bag that we had the bread in?'

'We threw it in the bin mate', I said. 'Fuck!' Jules replied, 'My money's in there!'

We went to the bin and it was empty. I asked Yono if he had emptied the bins. And he said that it had all gone to the rubbish tip outside. It was about five o'clock and we were getting ready to be locked in for the night. Jules was panicking.

The tip was a pile of rubbish from the whole prison. It was stored within a U-shaped concrete wall. They burned it off every second night and then a truck came and took away what remained. The chances of finding a brown paper bag in a rubbish tip were near impossible. Jules climbed on top of the pile of rubbish. There were flies everywhere and it stunk. Amazingly, he spotted a brown bag among the hundreds of brown bags and when he picked it up the money was inside. He was one lucky motherfucker to get that money back.

Another guy in Kerobokan had a similar experience to Jules and was set up by the police. Originally from Spain, David ran a property development company in Bali with his Indonesian partner. They worked together for three years before their relationship soured and he planted drugs in David's house and called the police. He had to pay 50,000 dollars to get only six months inside and made up a story that the drugs were for his medicinal use and he wasn't a dealer. Unfortunately, his lawyer also created a back-story to tell the prosecutors, but forgot to tell his client about it.

'Tell the court about your jet-ski accident', the prosecutor said to him in court.

David was dumbfounded. When he came back to Kerobokan and told us about it we couldn't stop ourselves from laughing. By the next day, we had invented his entire back-story for him. He was actually a jet-ski salesman with a Red Bull sponsorship, we said. He needed the drugs for his pain management because he had broken his leg in an accident, we said. 'When you go to court you should do a jet-ski "*vroom vroom*" action with your hands in front of the media', we told him, 'so they get it'.

We dragged it out all night.

While David was inside, his Indonesian partner took all of David's credentials and tried to transfer them to his name and then drain the bank account. Luckily, David had copies of all the original documents and his lawyer successfully blocked any moves by the former partner. The guy then disappeared because the police were after him for another matter.

David had all the proof that his former partner had fucked him over, had planted the drugs and tried to rip off his business but the Indonesian courts still threw him in jail for six months for not doing anything at all.

He's just another guy who was screwed by the Indonesian justice system.

CHAPTER 18

'INDOS'

I had the weirdest dreams in prison. Someone once remarked that inmates in Kerobokan needed a 'dream pillow'. When I asked what that was, they said it was a pillow that stored all your dreams at night so you could remember them and analyse them the following morning. It was an interesting concept, plugging your pillow into a computer and downloading your dreams.

In Kerobokan, I often wondered why certain dreams chose to pop up while I was so far from home.

The first dream was related to an event that happened while I lived in the States in October 1989. My uncle worked in the St Francis Hotel in San Francisco so a friend and I decided to catch a train from LA and take in an Oakland Raiders football match. We took a bus across the Oakland Bay Bridge and arranged to meet my uncle after work at his apartment before the game started.

The earthquake hit at about a quarter past five. The shaking started really slowly and got stronger and stronger to the point I thought I was going to die.

We were on a street called Geary Avenue in a three-story apartment, and everything started falling out of the cupboards and the whole building started to shake. We rushed downstairs and tried to exit through a gated door onto the street but the electricity was cut and the gate wouldn't open. I was standing there banging on the bars of the gate. I didn't want to be inside if the whole building came down on top of us.

In my dreams, I was shaking that gate again and it still wouldn't open.

Back in San Francisco in 1989, I put my hand through the gate and opened it from the outside. By that time everyone was outside standing on the street. We could hear the wail of fire engines and police cars, but we didn't know how bad the earthquake was until we saw it on the news that night. Thousands of people were injured and many people were killed when the Oakland Bridge collapsed.

Many dreams seemed to be based on memories from my time in the States. My Australian mate Glen came over to California when I was there and was working in a local liquor store. He was doing a shift by himself one Sunday and I popped in to see him. I was sitting at the end of the counter minding my own business and I didn't even see the other guy come into the shop. I actually heard the loud moan first, and when I looked up I saw Glen on his knees with a guy pointing a gun to his head. I locked on to the guy's shiny gun pointed at Glen's temple. The white punk on dope wearing a bandana yelled 'Give me the fucking money! Give me the fucking money!' Glen was doing his best to give him the fucking money while he was still down on his knees and I was saying to myself, 'Please don't shoot; don't shoot that gun'.

The fear I felt at that moment, and the image of that shiny gun, were burned into my brain.

All I could think about was what Glen's old man had said to him when he told him he was working in a liquor shop. 'You're crazy', Glen's dad had said. 'Someone will shoot you'. 'What the fuck will I tell his old man if it happens?' The robber then looked up and saw me and told me to get on the fucking ground, which I quickly did. The guy ran out of the store with the money and then people came running in to see if we were okay.

Me with two of Kerobokan's 'next top models' …
shirts off, sunglasses on, all while inside their room.

Right: One of the herb gardens being grown in a foam box at the back of the block. Anything that could make our meals taste better was highly valued.

Below left: Leftovers from a party inside our block. You could buy almost anything to drink inside prison, usually from the prison guards.

Below right: The bath in our room in Block B. Standing room only, and no hot water.

Dried fish that the Nigerians imported into the prison. Considered a delicacy in Africa, I couldn't bring myself to try them. I thought they were bats!

Above: A dried snake skin taken from one of the many snakes that slid through the blocksmat Kerobokan. One of the inmates in our block was going to make a belt out of it.

Below: A shoe rack in our block. Note the large green boots that belonged to one of the Nigerians. I gave my shoes to one of the Iranians when I left prison. I wouldn't have been allowed to carry them on the plane home they smelled so bad.

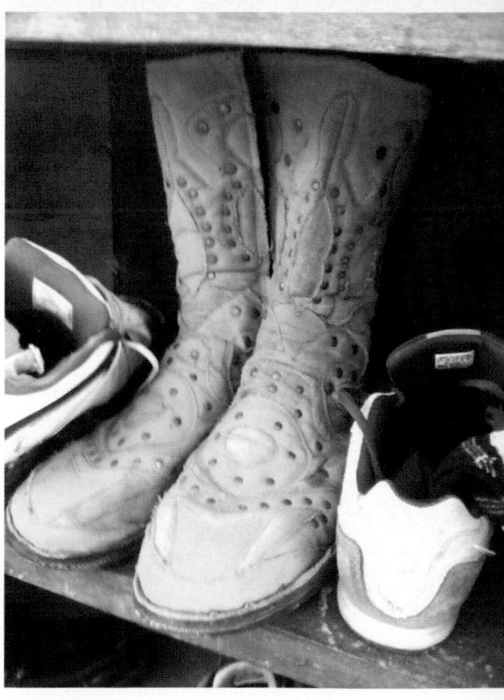

Above: Basil and I strike a pose at the gym.

Below: Our daily breakfast rations: five slices of bread, three eggs (alternating with a scoop of rice) and a piece of fruit.

Above: The front entrance to Kerobokan Prison, where hundreds of family, friends and curious tourists lined up in the heat to visit inmates such as the Bali Nine and Schapelle Corby.

Below: Basil with a Malaysian inmate.

Right: Our accident-prone 'chef' showing his injuries after another cooking disaster.

Below: Hamburger day at Kerobokan ... not quite the Aussie backyard barbeque but it would have to do.

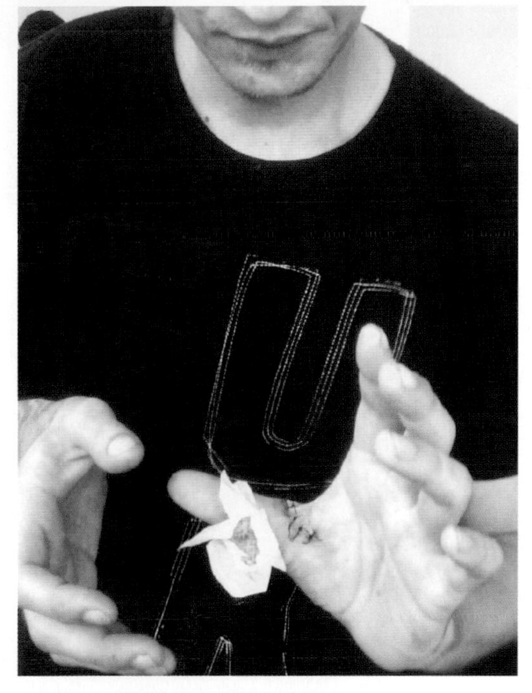

Free at last. Enjoying a cold beer at Sydney's Maroubra Beach. I would sit for hours and watch the ocean and the waves.

Later, some detectives came around to our house to show us photos of suspects and separately, we both picked out the same guy. The police arrested him and we later had to go to court and give evidence. We were sitting outside the courthouse with a cabbie who had also been robbed by the guy and he told us we were lucky. The punk had fired his gun at the cabbie after he had told him to start running. Fuck!

A final recurring dream was based on a time when I was in the States and I was arrested for driving under the influence of alcohol. Part of my probation was that I had to go to the morgue and see the effects drink driving had on others. The morgue staff were supposed to show me an autopsy of someone who had been killed in a car accident—either driving drunk or someone who had been killed by a drunk driver—and ram home the stupidity and selfishness of drink driving. I was determined to stand there and learn my lesson, no matter how shocking the scene was.

There was a body on the table with a sheet over it, but the body had a bulge on top of it. I took a closer look and when the morgue attendant removed the blanket, there was a baby curled up on her mother's stomach. Both were dead. Two days earlier, the young woman was pushing her baby in a pram and they were both killed in a drive-by shooting.

I saw that mother and child many times in my dreams in Kerobokan.

• • •

Life is cheap in Indonesia. On the TV news programs I watched in Kerobokan, they would show the bodies of murder victims or car crash victims with a crowd of locals taking photos of the ghastly scenes with their cameras and mobile phones. Bored, sweaty policemen would be there smoking their cigarettes and making no effort to shield the bodies from a willing media or a milling crowd, or even to protect the integrity of the crime scene for investigation.

There was no decorum or sense of dignity.

In June 2012, around the same time I had arrived in Bali, the body of 33-year-old Australian Mark Ovenden was discovered on the side of a rural road. A keen surfer and traveller who viewed Bali as a second home, Mark's body was found next to his motor scooter with his wallet still on him. Police originally regarded his death as an accident and it was only when the autopsy report came back that police and the family of the poor guy found out that he had actually been beaten and strangled.

I mention this tragic case only because it became entwined with my story in Denham Hitchcock's documentary 'Bali: The Dark Side of Paradise'. It also exemplifies the lack of support Australian families receive from DFAT—the Department of Foreign Affairs and Trade, which runs the Australian consulate in Indonesia—and the slapdash job the local police do in their investigations—issues I can fully relate to. It was good to see the Australian Foreign Affairs Minister Bob Carr get involved and request the Australian consulate put some pressure on the Balinese police investigation. I really hope the Ovenden family receives some answers and the cause of Mark's death is justly resolved, but the film I saw of Denham interviewing the inept police does not inspire a lot of confidence.

So you'll excuse me if my regard for the Indonesian people I met in Bali, the Kuta Police Station, Denpasar Court and Kerobokan Prison—the good-time girls and scammers, the corrupt police and justice system and the drugged and depraved locals spitting on the floor of the cell where they sat—seem somewhat coloured. The truth is, at different times during my year-long hell in Bali, I felt frustration, revulsion, anger and downright hatred towards them.

To make matters worse, in Block B, I was surrounded by Indonesians whose disgusting crimes would have led them to have had their throats slit if they had stayed in the other blocks. I met people whose crimes were so atrocious they belonged nowhere else but prison.

The Indonesian inmates were always scavenging or stealing from the *bule*s. They'd pretend they were just looking at food we were eating and ask, 'Can we try?' They'd circle like sharks when we were cooking or eating a meal. Then they'd stare at us when we ate like seagulls at a beach. They didn't dare walk up to us and ask for a cigarette, but would be happy to sit there just to watch us smoke.

After doing our laundry, we had to watch our clothes or they'd go missing, and days later we would see young Indonesians wearing our stuff. Bali Nine Michael's girlfriend brought him some new underwear in bright, fluorescent colours. He hung them all on the fence one day and came back in the afternoon to find they had all gone. The next day we were walking around the courtyard and, because the Indonesians always wore their shorts down around their hips and their underwear showing, we could see where Michael's underwear had ended up.

'Go and tell them you want them back', I told him. 'I don't want them back', Michael said, 'but at least I know who stole them'.

If you had good clothes, you had to just sit there and wait for them to dry otherwise they would 'walk' away. I learned that pretty quickly. I turned the designer T-shirts I had inside out so potential thieves wouldn't see the logos and would think it was a plain shirt. I asked Mario's girlfriend who worked in Myu's T-shirt business if she could make me a 'Hotel K' T-shirt. Although it didn't turn out as well as I hoped, I wore it around the prison with some pride. I washed all my clothes for a while but eventually I ended up paying a young inmate 10,000 rupiah to wash them and hang them out to dry. He would then sit there all day and watch them for me and bring them in.

Perhaps it was desperation that drove the Indonesian inmates to their actions. One of the Indonesians escaped when I was there because he heard his girlfriend had taken in a new lover at the house they once shared. The police later found him hiding in the bushes outside her house armed with a knife. The stupid thing was he had only three months left on his original sentence and yet he was willing to escape with the intent of murdering someone.

One of the Indonesians who slept beside me would often be wide- awake watching a movie at twelve o'clock at night. I kept asking him to turn the damn TV off and he would just stare at me, not understanding why. I complained to the other *bule*s about him and McQueen later told me he was in jail for raping a young girl. He was just a fucking doormat, laying there all day.

Despite struggling to understand the motivations and actions of most of the Indonesians I shared a block with, there were a few, however, who I grew to like. Andrew Chan took a young Indonesian kid under his wing and he spent a lot of time with him in the tower block. This young guy was pretty clueless and Andrew wanted to help him. The kid was due to be released soon and Andrew, who could speak a little Indonesian, asked him what he was going to do on the outside. The kid had no idea—most Indonesians are released with no money and just the clothes on their backs; it's no wonder so many walk straight back into crime—so Andrew let him cook in his kitchen. He then gave him 100,000 rupiah to get him started. 'If you don't have anywhere to stay, you can get a room and have some money to buy some food', Andrew explained to the guy. He then he gave the thankful kid another 100,000 just in case.

There was an old Indonesian guy who slept beside me on the floor of Block B. I never found out what he was inside for because he spoke next to no English that I could understand. He tended to keep to himself. But he saw me training in the gym one day and took a liking to me. I was doing some weights when I noticed he was watching me—his frail little body curled up in a ball of concentration. 'Come on', I said. 'Have a go!' but he just sat there and smiled, nodding his head.

One day, I caught him sitting down doing some forearm curls with the weights. 'Ahh!' I called out to him. 'You're a big boy now!'

After that he moved his mat a little closer to me. I don't know whether it made him feel safer or whether he just took a shining to me, but I could tell he was getting weaker as the months went on. I used to give him my banana and some bread in the morning and he would just laugh and nod his head. It was his way of saying thank you, I guess.

One night, he was laying perpendicular to me with our heads almost touching when he started shaking and making a grunting noise. As I rolled over to see what was wrong, an arm shot out in the dark and grabbed me really hard by the forearm and wouldn't let go. The heat that came out of that hand was unbearable. The old man was burning up.

I tried to sit up and saw in horror that there was foam

coming out of his mouth. When I looked at him I could tell he going to die. His face was grey and his body was a wet rag of perspiration. He kept holding on to me. I shouted for help and the boys called for a doctor, but it took an hour and a half for someone to come and there wasn't much we could do for him. We rolled him onto his side in the recovery position until the guards carried him out but I was sure he was already dead. I learned the next morning he had passed away.

I never felt sorry for myself for being in Kerobokan and I never shed a tear about my situation. But I have to admit I cried when the old man died. The guards wouldn't tell us what he died of because they were worried how we would react. All we wanted to know is was how contagious it was. A week later, when one of the Iranians dropped with the same symptoms and they took him off to hospital, we all started getting a little paranoid.

Tuberculosis was a real danger, more so than AIDS, as it's picked up through shared saliva and can be passed on through contaminated water or food, or just sitting next to someone who has it. We didn't know who had AIDS. Others pointed out people who had it, but I think out of a thousand people in Kerobokan there were probably only ten or fifteen that had it. The odds were slim.

Why did the old man grab my arm, I wondered. Was it for comfort, the presence of another solid form in the dark? Or was it just an involuntary movement? One of the other Indonesians in our block told me: 'He grabbed you to let you know he'll look after you from the afterlife. He wanted to thank you... you were good to him'.

I was the only *bule* he liked in Kerobokan.

CHAPTER 19

THE 'VET'

I wasn't scared of the Indonesian gangs because I was a *bule;* I didn't worry about the drug trade because I wasn't into that and I could look after myself in a fight. The gangs had access to weapons and the Internet, and at times I didn't know which was more dangerous. One of the Indonesian gang members showed me a website where you could order guns, grenades and other weapons and have them delivered to Kerobokan. I doubt they ever went to that extreme but it was a sobering thought and a prime example of the idiocy of life in an Indonesian prison where the gangs had the guards in the palms of their hands.

On top of the 120 dollars a month the Australians in Kerobokan receive from the Federal Government, an additional 100 dollars can also be spent on medical supplies. If inmates get sick, the consulate can get them the medicine they need, but only up to 100 dollars. The rest they have to pay for themselves.

The only thing that really scared me about being in Kerobokan was the idea of getting sick, because I had no financial support other than what my brother sent me from the States. I couldn't afford to get sick in prison.

The prison had a medical clinic attached to it that we called the 'Vet' because the standard of care there was barely above animal standard. The running joke in the prison was when you went to the clinic the staff there asked to you to 'open your mouth and bark'.

Jules went in to have his tooth removed and they started taking out the wrong one. He was livid. A Malaysian went to the clinic with a similar problem and they pulled his tooth out, gave him a cloth to chew on and sent him on his way. He was lying down on his mat afterwards and all of a sudden blood started pouring out of his mouth. They shifted him off to hospital and the doctors had to give him stitches. The so-called 'dentists' at Kerobokan just yanked out the tooth and then left the poor guy to his own devices.

I did a lot of boxing training with McQueen to keep my body healthy and my mind strong. One day it started raining heavily mid- way through and everyone ran for cover. Not me. I stood in the rain and finished my set. I didn't care if I got a little wet. The Indonesians just looked at me, totally perplexed.

The only problem was that our gym only had very small boxing pads and I had to curl my fingers over so they would fit in the gloves. Because of this I ended up breaking my finger three times and so had the pleasure of going to the 'Vet', where, true to its reputation, they did nothing for me. Then I dislocated a finger and they had to snap it back into place. It took a week to repair but it still fucking hurt.

I'd seen enough of the clinic to know I didn't want to go in there for anything more serious than a broken finger.

And then it happened. I became very ill with a stomach problem—a pain that just wouldn't go away. I thought I had appendicitis for a time and that I was going to die. It got to the point where I was really scared. I was eating rice but I didn't crap for a week. 'This is it,' I told myself. 'I'm fucked now'. I pissed orange for two weeks. I didn't know what was wrong with me.

'What is the worst case scenario?' I asked myself. 'They take you out in a body bag', was the answer that came back. Even then I was determined not to go to the prison clinic. By the end of the week I was relieved to be feeling much better, and I eventually recovered. After I was released I went to the doctor and he said I probably passed a kidney stone.

Despite the risk of injury, I boxed a lot in Kerobokan. It kept me fit and my mind sharp. While Myu and I were training we discovered a really promising Indonesian boxer named Clement. He had two fights before he went in the jail and struck us as someone who could be really successful on the outside. Myu and I decided to take him under our wing and see if we could help. I took some film of him boxing on my iPhone and told him I would show it around when I got out. Perhaps something would come of it. It would be a waste of talent if it didn't.

When I was on the bus going into Kerobokan I noticed a big Indonesian guy onboard with me. It's not something you see every day, a fat Indonesian, and I later found out his name was Adi. I asked him how much he weighed, which is not the smartest conversation starter when you're in handcuffs on a bus being taken to prison, but he didn't speak English anyway and he just smiled and nodded. He would have easily been over 100 kilograms.

Adi was watching me train in the gym one day so I raised my hands up and motioned to him did he want to do some boxing.

I called him over and he nodded that he would have a go. I was holding the pads up for him to hit and he was terrible. 'Come on', I teased him, 'put some effort into it'. He was so out of shape; he'd punch four or five times and he would be out of breath. I decided to see if I could get him into better shape. After two weeks, he was sustaining the workout for about three minutes and he was also able to do some of the skipping skills as well. Maybe I could make a boxer out of him.

'You're going well', I told him, trying to be as encouraging as possible. 'Your punches are getting harder too'. Adi couldn't understand what I was saying but he continued to smile and nod a lot. After six weeks, he was able to box in combination and really put a lot of power behind a punch. He was certainly also a lot fitter and slimmer than when I met him on the bus going to Kerobokan.

Around this time, an Indonesian gang member was bashed to death in his cell. The number one suspect was Adi. Had I inadvertently trained him so he could go out and kill someone who owed him a debt? Was he a drug rival? Or perhaps he just said the wrong thing to him one day? It was disturbing. Had he picked me out from the beginning? I thought he would be my 'project', but was I actually his? Allegedly, he told the guards the man 'fell' in the bathroom and hit his head on the sink. No charges were laid.

Adi was only in Kerobokan for a few months before being released. I looked into the visitors' room one day after he was released and he was sitting and laughing with all the guards. All the guards knew him and although he wasn't a gang member, all the gang bosses knew him and respected him as well. Who was he?

When Adi saw me, he came over bowing and nodding, with his hands together as if he was in prayer. I didn't even know he had been released. I gave him a tentative hug, but because he didn't speak English, there was no point confronting him about the rumours that he used my boxing lessons to get into shape and then kill someone in prison.

I tried not to ask too many questions.

We played a lot of sport in Kerobokan: tennis, basketball, badminton, soccer or just kicking a ball around. Joseph, one of the inmates at our block, was a tennis 'pro' at one of the Bali resorts and together with Bali Nine's Matthew he organised tennis tournaments. The winner received a small gift: a new towel. We played tennis almost every day, but the games were not as spirited as the volleyball tournament Chandra organised between the rival blocks.

We knew there was some betting going on behind the scenes about the outcome of some of the volleyball matches but we never got involved. We were just happy to form a team and play for pride—as much as you could get that in prison. We threw ourselves into the match, high-fiving every point, and we were well on top of our opponents. All of a sudden, Chandra started waving his arms around on the sidelines, pulling three of our players off the court and replacing them with three Indonesians from another block.

'What's going on here?' we complained. 'They play, they play', Chandra ordered. Mario and I told him to piss off... this is *our* team. Chandra insisted and he changed some of the players with outsiders. We walked off the court and the game was over. We didn't want to be party to any betting scam, nor did we want to be dictated to. We were *bule*s, and our sporting pride could not be compromised... especially in an Indonesian prison.

The Indonesians played soccer every afternoon for 50,000 rupiah a game, which is about 5 dollars. They split the money up between the team, which was usually six a side. The Indonesians loved beating the Westerners in soccer. They'd all be there on the sidelines cheering every illegal tackle. There were a lot of fights on field— pushing and shoving, settling the odd score with a head butt or trip—and that's why it was exciting to go out and watch. Invariably, the ball hit the razor wire on the back wall and went flat and the game was over.

The Nigerian, Emmanuel, kicked the ball over the wall and it struck the wooden cross on top of the church and it fell to the ground. Emmanuel was mortified; he too fell to the ground and started blessing himself.

A friend sent me over a rugby ball from Australia. That really reminded us of home. After kicking it back and forth in the oval, the temptation became too great and we started tackling each other. Other *bule*s joined it, and it became a three-on-three grudge match. The gangs came out of their block to watch us and it drew quite a crowd. Although the ground was hard and covered with rocks, we tackled each other, picked each other up and dumped each other on the hard ground. At the end of the game, our legs and arms were cut to shreds and bleeding. We had spent every ounce of our available energy in a stupid, pointless game and were thoroughly exhausted, but we never felt so alive.

McQueen and I were close—it was he who kept me

going a lot of the time inside—and it was difficult to think that it could well be many years until he saw the outside world again. One day, we were discussing the business we were eventually going to set up when he remarked that people back in Australia needed to hear about Kerobokan, what a hellhole it was and how corrupt the Indonesians were who were running it. I revealed to him that I wanted to do a documentary and that I was keen to write a book about my time in prison after I was released.

Mickey was very encouraging, and told me to make sure I followed through with all my plans when I got out of prison. One day, a long way into the future, he would get out too.

CHAPTER 20

LINDSAY

A British woman has described her ordeal in Bali's notorious Kerobokan Prison, the same jail where convicted Australian drug smuggler Schapelle Corby and the Bali Nine are serving time.

Rachel Dougall said she suffered savaged beatings within days of beginning a year-long sentence for drug- related crimes.

Dougall, 40, told the Daily Mail that she had a nervous breakdown after being locked up with drug addicts, HIV- positive inmates and sexually aggressive lesbians in a tiny cell at the prison, nicknamed 'Hotel K'.

'Most of the women were on drugs virtually every day', she said. 'If you had money the guards would get you anything you wanted. Inmates in the men's prison next door even paid prostitutes for overnight visits'.

The women's unit of Kerobokan where Dougall was locked up also houses Corby, who was sentenced to 20 years in 2005 after she was caught trying to smuggle 4.2 kilos of cannabis into the country in her boogie-board bag. She has always maintained her innocence.

According to friends and family, Corby's experience in the prison has led to her developing a mental illness. Since a judge ruled her sentence cut to 15 years, leading to the possibility of parole, she is reportedly doing much better. She is due to get out 2017.

Also held there are the so-called Bali Nine. The eight men and one woman were convicted in 2005 of attempting to traffic 8.3 kilos of heroin from Bali to Australia. Two of them, Myuran Sukumaran and Andrew Chan, still face death sentences and have appealed to President Susilo Bambang Yudhoyono for clemency.

Dougall was arrested after fellow Briton Lindsay Sandiford was caught at Bali's airport on a flight from Bangkok carrying a suitcase full of cocaine on May 19 last year. The 57-year-old grandmother's case made headlines after the judge ordered she be put to death via a firing squad.

Following her arrest Sandiford told police she had been forced to move the drugs after threats were made to her family by a drugs cartel. She implicated Dougall and two other men, one of them Dougall's partner, 44-year-old Julian Ponder, as her accomplices.

The other three were handed lesser sentences.

Sandiford's case has led to widespread outrage about Indonesia's harsh sentencing regime.

However, Dougall claimed to the Mail that Sandiford was 'pure evil' and 'not the innocent she would like people to believe'.

'Everyone thinks she's this poor naïve granny, but she's not. She doesn't deserve any sympathy; I've been told by many people in Bali and Britain that she's been bringing drugs into the country for 25 years'.

news.com.au, July 29, 2013

• • •

When I was awating sentencing in Denpasar, an English lady was also in the court. A lovely Australian lady named Virginia was sitting beside her for comfort and support. If I had met them on a bus in England I wouldn't have given them a second thought, but the lady was in handcuffs and this was Bali in 2012. Her name was Lindsay.

The British grandmother was detained at Denpasar International Airport in May 2012 trying to smuggle in 4.8 kilos of cocaine in her luggage after a flight from Bangkok. She implicated two other Englishmen, Julian Ponder and Paul Beales, in the crime but although a small amount of drugs were found at the house Julian shared with his girlfriend Rachel, and at the hotel where Paul was staying, prosecutors did not link the men to Lindsay's trafficking charge. Julian and Paul received six and four years in jail, respectively, for drug possession, but they will probably be out in three and a half. Julian's girlfriend Rachel Dougall received 12 months for allegedly concealing a crime. Lindsay, on the other hand, received 15 years at her pre-sentence hearing.

I'd read about her case when I was in the jail in Kuta and about the English guys who were implicated along with her. I read that she had requested through her lawyer to get a mattress because she couldn't sleep on the floor. I thought at the time, 'I'm lying on the floor. What makes you so special that you should get a mattress?'

But after I met her, I realised that Lindsay was a real person and not just a character to vilify and judge. How the fuck did a 57-year- old British grandmother end up in here? I travelled to court with Lindsay after I moved to Kerobokan and I could tell she was really struggling.

When I was at the courthouse, they held the women in one cell and the men in the other. People could come in and visit you while you were there. That's how I met Virginia, the woman who was supporting Lindsay. Virginia asked who I was and why I was there, and when I told her she just replied with a shocked, 'Oh, my God'. She said she'd come and sit in court with me. She said if I needed anything, just to let her know and she later brought me some toiletries—I didn't even have a toothbrush at this stage—and some food while I was in Kerobokan waiting to be sentenced.

In January 2013, about the same time I received my ten month sentence, Lindsay was given the death penalty for drug trafficking. Because she didn't have any money to pay off the prosecutor and judges, Lindsay took the fall for the drug smuggling charge despite the fact that 15 years was the pre-sentencing recommendation. How do you go from 15 years to death? Something was wrong there.

Lindsay was very disorientated and unfocused whenever I spoke to her. She was a big woman and looked older than her 57 years. She would change the subject quickly and it was hard to follow what she was saying but I remember the following exchange vividly. 'You know what they're going to do to me, don't you?' she offered one day when we were both on the prison bus going back to Kerobokan. She then put her finger to her head in the shape of a gun and fired. 'They're going to execute me. I'm dead'. I didn't know if she meant the Indonesian Justice system or the people she was in business with smuggling drugs.

Lindsay's defence was that she was an ordinary grandmother who got sucked into the drug trade and she only agreed to smuggle drugs into Bali because of threats to her family. Julian and Paul, whom she implicated in her case, were in my block and I got to know the two Brits pretty well during my time in Kerobokan. Without ever discussing their alleged involvement with Lindsay, Julian and Paul said that she wasn't the innocent victim she claimed to be. I went to court with Lindsay and I used to talk to her quite a bit so if that was the case, she certainly had me fooled.

Virginia was allowed into the prison to visit the female prisoners and give them moral support. When Lindsay came in to Kerobokan, Virginia helped her deal with her situation the best she could. I would also text Virginia and she would bring in food for me. She would drop off a food package to Lindsay, then I would ask Black Basil to give Lindsay the money and he would give me the bag of food Virginia had bought for me. I asked Basil to help because I didn't want to be seen in the women's block talking to Lindsay and have everyone back in my block asking me questions.

In August 2013, the Supreme Court rejected Lindsay's appeal against the death penalty. The UK government refused to finance an appeal or a review of her case because she had 'no reasonable prospect for success'. The courts had washed their hands of her.

The British press was all over the Lindsay Sandiford story. Journalists were sucked into the corrupt world of Kerobokan and were told they would have to pay the guards if they wanted the 'inside story'. They were falling over themselves trying to get to Lindsay and the Brits in our block. Julian and Paul refused to talk to the media, although Rachel tried to set the record straight when she was released in July 2013.

Julian and Pauly were good guys to have a drink with and I got along pretty well with them. Pauly was blind drunk in his top bunk one night and when he fell out of bed with a thud, everyone thought he was dead. But remarkably he just got up and walked away. I started calling him 'Drop Bear', after the infamous Australian myth told to many a tourist about carnivorous koala bears falling out of the trees in the night.

Because Kerobokan was going to be his home for the next couple of years Julian obviously wanted it to be as comfortable as possible, so he bought a water pump to improve the water pressure in the block. When he and Paul moved in it would take half a day just to fill a basin of water. Julian also hired an Indonesian guy to be his 'gofer', to do his shopping on the outside, to bring in alcohol and whatever else he needed.

Now there is talk someone wants to make a film about Lindsay's case. One of the Brits told me from Kerobokan: 'Paul, they're going to make a movie about us and you're going to be in it too'.

'Wonderful', I said, underwhelmed. 'Only if I can play myself.'

'My people will call your people', he said.

I will be waiting quite a while for that call.

CHAPTER 21

WHAT I MISSED, WHAT I LOST AND WHAT I GAINED

Each morning in Kerobokan, I would lie on a huge concrete slab at the back of the prison because the concrete was cool after the previous night. We'd put our mattresses out there during the day to dry because we would sweat so much during the night. Each morning, the mattresses would be drenched. Lying on my back, I would watch planes flying overhead and I would think to myself, 'I can't wait to get on that plane and get the fuck out of here'.

In prison, planes can be a silent killer. Seeing a plane flying overhead could crush you emotionally and leave you depressed for the entire day. When I got out of prison one of the first things I did was to sit on the beach and stare at the horizon. I would watch the ocean for hours on end, taking in the sound of the beach and the surf.

It got to the point, however, that I stopped looking skyward and at planes taking off from nearby Denspasar Airport in case I upset one of the guys who were in prison for life. Because so many of the prisoners were high on drugs, you didn't know how they would react to a gesture like that, or an innocent word said at the wrong time. I spent hours observing the other inmates in the outside courtyard. I watched people all the time—how they moved, where they were heading and the look on their faces—just in case there were any sudden movements. I also studied them because it fascinated me to watch their daily moodswings and to see their psychological conditions. Some deteriorated, some were just lost, some had given up hope.

I always had my back up against a wall so I could see everyone in front of me.

After I was released I was contacted by Kathryn Bonella. Kathryn is the best-selling author of *Schapelle Corby: My Story*, *Hotel Kerobokan* and *Snowing in Bali*—three books that expose the dark side of Bali. When she heard about what had happened to me, Kathryn rang me to encourage me to talk and write about my story. She could relate to the frustration I faced at the corruption of the Indonesian justice system and could fully understand why I refused to play their game of extortion and decided to take my chances in Kerobokan.

During our many discussions, it was Kathryn who finally asked the question that had been buried in the back of my mind all this time. 'Do you think you were set up?' I have thought about it often. It was possible Icha, the girl I met before I was arrested, could have set me up to have me robbed and then arrested. I just don't know.

But considering what I went through—what I missed and lost from my ten months in prison—the prospect that I could have been targeted from the start would be the ultimate insult.

My time in Kerobokan was like putting my life on pause for ten months. Days just blurred into one. I spent a whole hour one day watching a cat walk along the fence. One morning I watched a line of ants crawl up a wall carrying crumbs many times larger than their bodies. How the fuck did they do that?

I never contemplated trying to escape. I only had ten months to serve so why bother? Most of the other people in Kerobokan had contemplated escape at one time or another. It could very easily have been done. There were only a couple of guards at the back of the prison and you could see the traffic zipping past in the breaks in the wall that hadn't been rebuilt since the 2012 riot. Many inmates think about it, but few actually try to escape. The prison guards caught an Indonesian trying to escape in a dumpster bin and flushed him out by setting it alight, leaving him badly burnt.

Being confined to one place, in a space that was hot as hell and often as uncompromising, sometimes brought out the best in people.

The poor Indonesian who was set alight for trying to escape in a dumpster was left with terrible burns that wouldn't heal. The medical clinic inside the prison couldn't treat him and there wasn't a chance in hell they would send the poor guy to a public hospital, so Michael had his girlfriend and his mother bring in aloe vera cream for the guy's injuries. Little things like that in Kerobokan went a long way to shining the light on the innate decency of people—no matter their mistakes, no matter their crimes.

McQueen received a reward of sorts from the karma police after I left the prison. I don't know whose idea it was to have a boxing tournament—perhaps it was McQueen's himself—but to no surprise he won. He was the best fighter in the prison. I heard during the tournament he tore a biceps muscle and had to go to hospital in Denpasar. McQueen had complained to the Australian consulate for some time that he needed a knee operation as well and they agreed to do both procedures at the same time. Although he would have been in a lot of pain, the chance to sleep in a comfortable bed, have a warm shower and a decent meal would have been worth it.

I realised that a distance of 15 metres—the distance between a crumbling white external wall and where you stood trapped inside—separated you from the person you really are. Who was I on the outside? I tried to look at myself in the mirror and not ask myself why I was there, but my time in prison ultimately forced me to confront some real issues in my life. An errant son, a distant brother, a serial partner and a part-time father, and although I wasn't a criminal or a drug addict, I was careful within reason not to judge anyone else by the crimes they had committed.

I missed so many things being in Kerobokan: a glass of fresh milk, a cold drink of pure water, a meat pie. Cheese! What I would have given to enjoy a Subway sandwich in prison, or spaghetti bolognaise or real Mexican food, or the smell of a woman's perfume.

I may have lost ten months of life but I know I also gained a lot too. I programmed my mind before I went into prison that I was going to do four years and that's why I got through ten months. Going in to Kerobokan I convinced myself I could even have done Schapelle Corby's sentence, but it was enough to give me the wake-up call I needed in my life. When I finally finished my time, I realised I could put my mind to anything and achieve it.

I learned to share with everyone, even people I didn't particularly like. 'If I have, I will give', I used to say to anyone who asked me for a cigarette, or food or clothing. I couldn't hold a grudge against anyone for more than a couple of days. There was no point holding on to anger in prison.

I am also sure that in some small way I was able to help some of the members of the Bali Nine. Because I am older than the younger guys, I was looked on as a father figure to some of them and a big brother to some of the others. I didn't know any of them from a bar of soap when I walked into Kerobokan and they didn't know me. But I grew to know them and love some of those guys as people.

Maybe I was destined to go into Kerobokan all along and meet them; maybe help them a little bit and be there for them if they needed someone on the inside to talk to... someone like me who knew what they were going through. Did I ever think I would end up in prison and meet the Bali Nine and share Christmas lunch with Schapelle Corby? Hell no. It was a bizarre set of circumstances that put me there in the first place.

Most importantly, I gained some much-needed meaning in my life.

As I came to the end of my time in Kerobokan prison I wondered what my fate would be. In the end, and without any notice, Indonesian immigration just turned up one day ready to deport me. I hadn't even packed. 'You're supposed to give me a time to tell me when you're coming in', I told them. They were rushing me out.

Then I remembered I had to get my phone with all my pictures on it. 'No, you come now', they said.

I didn't even get a chance to say goodbye to many of the guys in Block B. I caught McQueen in the common area as I was gathering up my things and he couldn't even look at me when I tried to say goodbye. As I came to the end of my time there, I didn't make a huge fuss about the fact I would soon be leaving. It wasn't wise to wave that in front of the face of people serving 10 years to life in prison. But Mickey had been a good friend and I tried to find the words to say goodbye. He didn't want to hear them anyway.

'See you', Mickey said as he turned and walked away as I approached. There was no man-hug, no bro-hug or shaking of hands. And very quickly, he was gone.

Indonesian immigration was trying to drag me out of jail but I wasn't leaving until I got my phone card. I went into the front office with one of the gang members I knew and asked the guard on duty if I could get my sim card out of my phone. There was another guard there and he grabbed all the phones and put them on a desk. I sorted through them and picked one up and the guard who was in charge said, 'No, that's not yours. Yours is a Mito', so he knew which I one I was looking for. I pulled the cover off the phone and because he was watching me, I grabbed the memory card with my thumb and palmed it as I clicked the sim card out of the phone.

Most of those photos of my time inside Kerobokan used in the Channel 9 documentary and in this book were on that chip.

After I gathered all my belongings, I couldn't wait to leave Kerobokan. As the front door to the prison opened, a great ray of light hit my face and people from Indonesian immigration whisked me away to the airport. Channel 9 was also there with a film crew and caught the whole thing on camera.

Also waiting for me was Michelle.

CHAPTER 22

COMING HOME

Bali – they call it the Island of the Gods. It's exotic, enchanting, and its Australia's favourite holiday destination. So what's not to love about it?

Plenty, as 'Bali: The Dark Side of Paradise' will reveal on Sunday, July 21, 2013 at 8.30 p.m. in a Nine

Network special presentation hosted by reporter Denham Hitchcock.

From the moment you step off the plane, Bali is a sensory overload. From the sweaty chaos of the streets where designer stores compete with pushy hawkers to the air-conditioned luxury of the resorts it's a grand bazaar of sights, smells and sounds framed by Bali's famous beaches, with some of the world's best surfing.

It's not surprising that one million Aussies visit Bali every year. But there's another statistic you won't read about in the guidebooks: the number of Australians injured and killed in Bali. In fact one Australian dies there every nine days.

Many of these deaths are from misadventure, especially drownings and motorbike accidents. But there's another, far more sinister side to this tourist paradise – the robberies, the shocking rapes and the murders.

Bali is a shadowy world where sometimes it's hard to know who is the criminal and who's the victim.

In this Nine Network special, we take viewers inside the feared Kerobokan Prison, where you'll see for the first time what it's really like for Australians behind the razor wire … the drugs, the weapons, the wild parties – and just what it takes to stay alive.

Denham Hitchcock shows you Bali as you've never seen it, the other side, the dark side of Australia's most popular holiday playground.

Channel 9 Promotion: July 2013.

• • •

'Hotel K' has become a real tourist spot, with ordinary Aussies lining up for hours in the heat, taking photos of the prison or chatting aimlessly to each other about their holiday. The visitors' room is barely 10 metres wide by 20 metres long, but it accommodates hundreds of people at a time, all clambering for a place to sit with their loved ones or with people they've only seen before on TV.

I used to go to the visitors' room even when I didn't have visitors and sit with some of the people waiting to see the Bali Nine. When the Bali Nine first came into the prison, visitors used to fight for their place in the line and I am sure, at first, the boys especially appreciated the interest being shown in them so far away from home. Andrew, Myu and Matthew were okay—they appreciated the gifts and people's prayers and good wishes—but some of the others couldn't even get out of bed to go and say hello. When I saw Andrew carrying bags of goods under both arms that visitors had given him, I remarked it was like the Easter Show.

One of the younger members of the Bali Nine, however, had worked it all out to a fine art. Just before the guards sounded the buzzer to end the visiting session, he would come out to receive his money and gifts, and then disappear back inside.

Elvis had left the building.

When I was drinking in bars in Bali before my arrest, I would hear people talk about visiting the Bali Nine. 'I'm going to take some food to them tomorrow', I'd hear. 'I know the Bali Nine and they live like kings'.

Well, that's not true, unless you call sweating it out in a poorly ventilated cell with a death sentence hanging over your head 'living like a king'. When I was in Kerobokan, I remarked to Si Yi one day, 'You must get a lot of visitors here', and he said, 'not really'. It doesn't happen as often as you think, for him. Talk is cheap.

The entire prison system in Bali is not only corrupt, it's also incompetently run. When the Indonesians finish their sentences in Kerobokan, they're still in there three months later waiting for the paperwork to be processed from Jakarta. Their sentence is up but they can't leave prison because the paperwork hasn't come through quickly enough. A prisoner can spend another six to twelve weeks in Kerobokan because the Indonesian officials are too useless to process the release of their own countrymen.

The Indonesian government are keen to deport *bule*s straight after their sentence is finished, but if the right people haven't been paid, they too can be held up in immigration for weeks on end, as my friend Jules discovered.

When I was released from prison, Michelle arranged to travel back with me to Australia. It was all premeditated; the relationship we had was already formed in her head. I can pick them a mile away.

I asked Michelle to get me a backpack in which to put the few things I owned. One of the Ugandans had tried to sell me his travel bag before I left, but it was the bag with which he was caught smuggling drugs into Denpasar Airport and I thought that would be bad luck. Mickey McQueen also warned me to be careful, half- jokingly, saying that the bag had so many hidden compartments, it probably still had drugs in it. No thank you.

When I left Kerobokan, I was able to fit all my possessions in a small backpack. I arrived in Sydney in shorts, sandals and a T-shirt in the middle of winter, absolutely freezing.

I told Michelle I would pay her back for all the things she bought me. She waited with me for three hours until I was cleared to go home. Immigration was supposed to escort me onto the flight but as soon as I walked through customs and they checked my paperwork they said I was free to go.

'Aren't you going to watch me get on the plane?' I asked. The customs official said he trusted me. I went and sat in the bar and had a cold beer and a nice meal. It was too soon to reflect on my experience and, in a perverse sort of way, I was sorry to be leaving so many friends behind. I had found some meaning in my life and the relationships I formed with people in Kerobokan were real and purposeful. I knew where I was heading and what I needed to do to get my life back on track, but what was to become of them?

In the end, the New Zealand consulate came through for me. I got my New Zealand passport renewed because I could show I had a ticket back to Auckland. My brother Dave bought the ticket for me, with a stopover in Sydney so I could sort out my resident's visa, and I was out of there. What had been a stumbling block all through my time in

Bali—my ongoing visa issues—quickly dissipated and I was home again. Home in Australia.

I told Michelle I was going to stay with the mother of the girlfriend of one of the Bali Nine in Melbourne and she became upset that I wasn't going to go home with her. I met up with Hamish Thompson from Channel 9 after I cleared customs in Sydney, and because I felt guilty I asked him if I could go to Michelle's place in Brisbane after we concluded the interviews for Denham Hitchcock's documentary 'Bali: The Dark Side of Paradise'. I thought I owed that much to her for supporting me through the last weeks of my prison sentence.

The interview with Channel 9 went well although Hamish was a little preoccupied because Nelson Mandela was apparently on his death-bed and Hamish had to be ready to drop everything at a moment's notice (Mandela rallied, and hung on until the end of the year). They rushed through the process without any negotiation about what my story was worth. When I broached the subject, I was told to wait a couple of weeks and Channel 9 would get back to me with an offer, which they finally did. I gave them all the images and film from my camera, but I emphasized to them that there was some material on there they couldn't use as it identified other prisoners who did not want to be on film.

The documentary that aired on Channel 9 at the end of July 2013 destroyed the credibility of the prison. Jakarta went nuts. After the TV program went to air, the Indonesian authorities did another sweep of the prison searching for phones and laptops. I received texts from inside prison saying 'WTF! We're getting smashed in here!' They came down hard on the prisoners because of the photos and videos I had smuggled out. I felt bad about that and I believe Channel 9 should have consulted me more before my story went to air.

I went to Brisbane and stayed with Michelle because I had nowhere else to go. Michelle, who had a couple of adult children, lived with her mother in Deception Bay and rented a place next door for us to live in. I could see where this was heading. It was moving too fast. I also thought it was quite ironic... I was jailed in Kerobokan Prison for fraud and deception and I ended up in Deception Bay after I was released. The truth was, I was still deceiving myself. This was not a relationship I wanted to pursue.

Michelle was planning trips to stay in hotels together and go to see Fleetwood fucking Mac. 'That's all great', I told her, 'but I have no money. How are we going to pay for all this?' She even bought a TV for me, and clothes and shoes. 'Don't buy me anything', I told her. 'I don't need anything'. Having lived in Kerobokan for the best part of a year, I had learned to travel light and discard what I didn't need. I didn't want to start accumulating possessions again.

Michelle worked in the mines in Queensland and was away for a couple of weeks at a time. While she was away I took the opportunity to travel up to Queensland's Fraser Coast, about three hours away, to visit the mother of one of my old Qantas mates. I had known Tony's mother all through my teenage years and it was great to reconnect with her. Michelle's stepfather offered to take me up there and Michelle met me at the end of the week and brought me back to her mother's place.

I was trying hard to find a job. I could have got work as a car salesman but I had to pay 600 dollars for a license in Queensland and I just didn't have the money. I even started going door-to-door to look for work in Brisbane I was so desperate.

Michelle was running out of money and then she started getting angry at me. 'You need to get a job', she said to me. 'I'm trying', I told her. She went away to work in the mines again and I realised I was happy she was gone. Whenever she came back, it felt like I was in an unhappy marriage. I had exchanged one prison for another and I realised I had to get out of there.

The day before she got back home from the mines, I packed up all my stuff and I decided to leave. I was packing my bags into a taxi when her stepfather pulled up in his car. He was on the phone to Michelle straight away.

Michelle immediately rang me. 'Where the fuck do you think you're going?' she demanded. I told her I was going back to live in Sydney, but I was actually heading north back to Queensland's Fraser Coast. I should have sat her down and had a long conversation with her, but my head was spinning and I just couldn't take the aggravation of an intense relationship straight out of prison. Not that Michelle was in any mood to listen to me.

Michelle tracked me down at Queensland's Fraser Coast and abused the shit out of me. Her mum sent a letter to Tony's mother who had said I could stay with her and clear my head a little, stating I was an 'evil, evil man' who couldn't be trusted. Thankfully, Tony's mum didn't believe her. 'That's not the Paul I know', she told me. It was great to have someone who believed in me.

Michelle wanted me to pay for her airfares to Bali; she was a 'humanitarian' she said and I was just a 'scumbag'. Her bill from phoning me when I was in prison was over 1,000 dollars and she wanted me to pay for it because I encouraged her to call. I didn't ask her to speak for two hours!

Michelle threatened to tell the Bali Nine and others inside Kerobokan that I'd 'fucked them over'. It wasn't true, but I freaked out. After the documentary aired, I started getting death threats allegedly from some of the people still inside who weren't happy their photos were shown on screen. They had seen the documentary on the Internet. 'I told them where you are!' Michelle screamed down the phone, 'and you deserve what they are going to do to you, you piece of shit!'

I became increasingly paranoid. I had just started work and I was trying to build a new life for myself. All of my possessions were in storage in Sydney after I let my apartment lease lapse when I was in Kerobokan and I had no way of paying for anything. I would have to pay thousands of dollars to get them back, but you know what? I didn't need them anymore. They reminded me too much of my old life and I was happy to let them go... the clothes, the furniture and all my worldly possessions I had up until I went into prison.

I also agonised over whether to write this book. I didn't want to do anything to jeopardise the appeals of the Bali Nine or make conditions in Kerobokan any tougher for the *bule*s.

I was still in two minds when I received a text message from an old friend. It was Mickey McQueen.

'Do the book', he wrote. 'Blow the fucking lid off the place'.

EPILOGUE

When I was in Kerobokan, I jotted down some notes about certain events that became the basis of this book. This is how I expressed the feelings I was experiencing: 'Frustration, starvation, perspiration, overpopulation, hallucination, traumatisation, vermination, infestation, deprivation, dehydration, detoxification, captivation, alienation, isolation, ventilation, backwardation, umbilication... no refrigeration!'

It took me some time to readjust to life on the outside. Although I put on five kilos in the first week, it took me quite a while for me to regain my health and settle back into a better sleep pattern. I would wake up in the middle of the night always around the same time—I don't know how many times I saw the time 1.11 a.m. click over on my bedside clock—and realise I wasn't in prison anymore. I am back training and I believe a healthy lifestyle is important—a healthy body, a healthy mind.

In the years after I said goodbye to Kerobokan, I straightened my personal life out and settled on Queensland's Fraser Coast. A friend recommended me to a local company where I found work in sales. They are great people to work for.

I am glad to say there is a new lady in my life, someone who knows of my time in Kerobokan at the courtesy of the

Indonesian justice system. I reconnected with my mother in the States as she slowly regained her health and regularly talk and email my brother, who has created a fine life for himself over there and left the troubles of his youth far behind him.

I don't know what my father thinks of my 'experience' in Bali because I haven't spoken to him about it. I try not to reflect on the fact that he didn't try to contact me when I was in prison and, if he did know about my situation, why he didn't offer to help. Our relationship is complicated, I guess... I don't know what I would say to him if I met him but one day, we'll sit down and talk it all through. One day.

I often think about those who are still in Kerobokan—McQueen and the other bules from around the globe; Matty, Michael and Scotty Rush from the Bali Nine. I look forward to sitting with Mickey McQueen with a cooler full of coronas on a beach somewhere enjoying two fat Cuban cigars one day soon. Schapelle Corby was sentenced to 20 years and only served 9 years and 4 months in prison, so anything is possible.

I set up a charity, 'Foundation 9', to try to help the Bali Nine in prison. I wrote to many companies, not asking for money, but for products such as clothing, toiletries and furniture, that could be donated to the Bali Nine in prison. Not new or expensive items, but discontinued brands or out of date items... anything that would make their lives in prison a little more comfortable.

I didn't receive a single reply or offer.

It was perhaps naïve of me—the Bali Nine are convicted drug traffickers and, as such, don't deserve our sympathy—but they are still people; young men who made a terribly poor decision and who may still pay for that with their lives.

If they had been arrested in Australia, they would have received between 7 and 12 years—far less than the 20 years, life in jail and the death penalty they received—not that that negates what they did.

The respective members of the Bali Nine dealt with many issues in Kerobokan—personal, emotional and health issues I have alluded to in this book but haven't detailed because I don't want anything to impact on their lives other than trying to help them in what remains a difficult environment—an environment I shared with them and experienced firsthand. They need counselling, and I believe the Australian Government should be doing more to help them other than giving them 120 dollars a month, handing out drugs like Xanax and buying them a DVD player.

Their story has the potential to educate young people about the dangers of drugs and I don't believe they need to languish or die in prison to ram that story home. It has now been more than a dozen years since they were captured.

Time is a surreal concept in Kerobokan and when you've stopped counting days, hours and minutes a transition is made to the acceptance of the helpless reality inside Block B. Time means nothing anymore. It's not that you give up on life but you can feel hope slowly slipping away.

Andrew Chan never gave up on life ... he held firm that he would live. In his own way, Andrew, had grown accustomed to his circumstances. Despite the pointlessness of his situation, he managed to create a compassionate air and gave much of his time to listen to people. Being embraced by his unwavering positivity, despite his own situation, helped to dispel the fear that welled inside me in those early days in prison.

Now that I am on the outside, I have voiced my opinion about the hypocrisy of the system. How could Andrew and Myu be on death row for smuggling drugs when drugs were so freely available in the prison? In all the time I knew Andrew, he never took drugs but he did have a generous nature. Through his eyes he saw inmates as people; they were human and not the sum of their deeds. If they were suffering, he would generously share money donated to him with those who needed it the most.

This was the man I knew.

With executions looming in April 2015, I watched the news with a heavy heart. All I could think was surely this won't happen. I'd always believed in my heart that they would not be executed. I tried to imagine how Andrew was feeling, the years of trauma and waiting that he endured as a model prisoner. So many thoughts, and feelings of anger, filled me. I would send messages to him often, letting him know I was out here but I was also with him in there. As the execution date neared, however, the umbilical cord was cut to say goodbye to my friend and I could only follow events via the media.

There is one more thing that needs to be said. I wonder if the fighter jets buzzing over Kerobokan, the armoured vehicle escorts, the press photographers, the 'selfie' taken on the flight to the execution site with Andrew and Myu were all a show of power by the Indonesians? The Indonesian Government were very deliberate and calculating in regards to announcing the original date of the execution as ANZAC Day.

Four days later, on 29th of April 2015, eight men faced the firing squad. It was as if the universe was talking to me…

"29", two of the Bali Nine were going to their deaths.

The eight condemned men embraced each other with courage, held hands in a line of strength, and sang Amazing Grace. His blindfold still off, Andrew allegedly looked the soldiers in the eye, as if to say, "After you shoot me, you're dismissed." Covered by plain white sheets, their blood replicated the red and white Indonesian flag.

I would love to go back to Bali and visit the guys in Kerobokan, but I know that is impossible. I doubt if I would be allowed through customs and, if I was, my safety there couldn't be guaranteed. My feelings toward the Indonesian people have softened—many are trapped in a poverty cycle in what remains predominantly a third- world country—but I have nothing but contempt for the Indonesian justice system.

My story, I hope, will be a cautionary tale for travellers who take the beauty of Bali for granted and don't realise how quickly things can go wrong. Recently, tonnes of rubbish, paper waste and plastic bottles were flushed down Bali's water system and closed the main tourist beaches on the island. Champion surfer Kelly Slater has stated that Bali's beaches will be unsurfable in five years' time. The island is disintegrating from the inside out because of poor planning, apathy and corruption.

Just like its justice system.

What did I learn from my experience? I look at my life now, and I realise material possessions aren't important anymore. Buying nice things won't make you happy on their own. I survived with the clothes on my back in Kuta Police Station and then had pulled everything together that I needed to survive from next to nothing once I was inside Kerobokan. I realise I don't need too many things now to be happy and live comfortably.

Spending almost 300 days in prison also taught me who my real friends were. Many so-called friends have fallen by the wayside in the past year and my real friends—they know who they are— still play an important role in my life. I'm also making many new friends, forming new, healthy relationships and living the life I hoped to live while I was in prison.

I've finally put the past behind me.

ABOUT ALAN WHITICKER

Alan Whiticker is the best-selling author of almost 40 books, including *Wanda: The Untold Story of the Wanda Beach Murders* (2003), *12 Crimes That Shocked the Nation* (2005), and *The Satin Man: Uncovering the Mystery of the Missing Beaumont Children* (2013). A former teacher and university lecturer, he is now an author and commissioning editor with New Holland Publishers.

This edition published in 2017
First published in 2014 by New Holland Publishers
London • Sydney • Auckland

The Chandlery, 50 Westminster Bridge Road, London SE1 7QY, United Kingdom
1/66 Gibbes Street, Chatswood, NSW 2067, Australia
5/39 Woodside Avenue, Northcote, Auckland 0627, New Zealand

newhollandpublishers.com

A record of this book is held at the British Library and the National Library of Australia.

ISBN 9781921024702

Managing Director: Fiona Schultz
Publisher: Alan Whiticker
Designer: Keisha Galbraith
Cover Designer: Catherine Meachen
Project Editor: Emily Carryer
Production Director: Olga Dementiev
Printer: Hang Tai Printing Company Limited

10 9 8 7 6 5 4 3 2 1